MznLnx

Missing Links Exam Preps

Exam Prep for

Corporate Management, Governance, and Ethics Best Practices

Vallabhaneni, 1st Edition

The MznLnx Exam Prep is your link from the texbook and lecture to your exams.
The MznLnx Exam Preps are unauthorized and comprehensive reviews of your textbooks.

All material provided by MznLnx and Rico Publications (c) 2010
Textbook publishers and textbook authors do not particpate in or contribute to these reviews.

MznLnx

Rico
Publications

Exam Prep for Corporate Management, Governance, and Ethics Best Practices
1st Edition
Vallabhaneni

Publisher: Raymond Houge
Assistant Editor: Michael Rouger
Text and Cover Designer: Lisa Buckner
Marketing Manager: Sara Swagger
Project Manager, Editorial Production: Jerry Emerson
Art Director: Vernon Lowerui

Product Manager: Dave Mason
Editorial Assitant: Rachel Guzmanji
Pedagogy: Debra Long
Cover Image: Jim Reed/Getty Images
Text and Cover Printer: City Printing, Inc.
Compositor: Media Mix, Inc.

(c) 2010 Rico Publications

ALL RIGHTS RESERVED. No part of this work covered by the copyright may be reproduced or used in any form or by an means--graphic, electronic, or mechanical, including photocopying, recording, taping, Web distribution, information storage, and retrieval systems, or in any other manner--without the written permission of the publisher.

Printed in the United States
ISBN:

For more information about our products, contact us at:
Dave.Mason@RicoPublications.com

For permission to use material from this text or product, submit a request online to:
Dave.Mason@RicoPublications.com

Contents

CHAPTER 1
   INTRODUCTION   1
CHAPTER 2
   CORPORATE-GOVERNANCE BEST PRACTICES   10
CHAPTER 3
   CORPORATE-ETHICS BEST PRACTICES   30
CHAPTER 4
   GENERAL-MANAGEMENT BEST PRACTICES   39
CHAPTER 5
   MANUFACTURING- AND SERVICE-MANAGEMENT BEST PRACTICES   49
CHAPTER 6
   MARKETING- AND SALES-MANAGEMENT BEST PRACTICES   60
CHAPTER 7
   QUALITY-MANAGEMENT BEST PRACTICES   70
CHAPTER 8
   PROCESS-MANAGEMENT BEST PRACTICES   83
CHAPTER 9
   HUMAN-RESOURCES MANAGEMENT BEST PRACTICES   91
CHAPTER 10
   ACCOUNTING, TREASURY, AND FINANCE-MANAGEMENT BEST PRACTICES   101
CHAPTER 11
   INFORMATION-TECHNOLOGY MANAGEMENT BEST PRACTICES   111
CHAPTER 12
   INTERNATIONAL-BUSINESS MANAGEMENT BEST PRACTICES   120
CHAPTER 13
   PROJECT-MANAGEMENT BEST PRACTICES   127
ANSWER KEY   135

TO THE STUDENT

COMPREHENSIVE

The *MznLnx* Exam Prep series is designed to help you pass your exams. Editors at MznLnx review your textbooks and then prepare these practice exams to help you master the textbook material. Unlike study guides, workbooks, and practice tests provided by the texbook publisher and textbook authors, *MznLnx* gives you **all** of the material in each chapter in exam form, not just samples, so you can be sure to nail your exam.

MECHANICAL

The MznLnx Exam Prep series creates exams that will help you learn the subject matter as well as test you on your understanding. Each question is designed to help you master the concept. Just working through the exams, you gain an understanding of the subject--its a simple mechanical process that produces success.

INTEGRATED STUDY GUIDE AND REVIEW

MznLnx is not just a set of exams designed to test you, its also a comprehensive review of the subject content. Each exam question is also a review of the concept, making sure that you will get the answer correct without having to go to other sources of material. You learn as you go! Its the easiest way to pass an exam.

HUMOR

Studying can be tedious and dry. MznLnx's instructional design includes moderate humor within the exam questions on occassion, to break the tedium and revitalize the brain

Chapter 1. INTRODUCTION

1. _____ is the process of comparing the cost, cycle time, productivity, or quality of a specific process or method to another that is widely considered to be an industry standard or best practice. Essentially, _____ provides a snapshot of the performance of your business and helps you understand where you are in relation to a particular standard. The result is often a business case for making changes in order to make improvements.
   a. Cost leadership
   b. Competitive heterogeneity
   c. Complementors
   d. Benchmarking

2. A _____ is the belief that there is a technique, method, process, activity, incentive or reward that is more effective at delivering a particular outcome than any other technique, method, process, etc. The idea is that with proper processes, checks, and testing, a desired outcome can be delivered with fewer problems and unforeseen complications. _____s can also be defined as the most efficient (least amount of effort) and effective (best results) way of accomplishing a task, based on repeatable procedures that have proven themselves over time for large numbers of people.
   a. Best practice
   b. Design management
   c. Hierarchical organization
   d. Fix it twice

3. _____ generally refers to a list of all planned expenses and revenues. It is a plan for saving and spending. A _____ is an important concept in microeconomics, which uses a _____ line to illustrate the trade-offs between two or more goods.
   a. 33 Strategies of War
   b. 28-hour day
   c. 1990 Clean Air Act
   d. Budget

4. _____ is the acquisition of goods and/or services at the best possible total cost of ownership, in the right quality and quantity, at the right time, in the right place and from the right source for the direct benefit or use of corporations, individuals generally via a contract. Simple _____ may involve nothing more than repeat purchasing. Complex _____ could involve finding long term partners - or even 'co-destiny' suppliers that might fundamentally commit one organization to another.
   a. Sole proprietorship
   b. Golden parachute
   c. Procurement
   d. Psychological pricing

5. A _____ or business method is a collection of related, structured activities or tasks that produce a specific service or product (serve a particular goal) for a particular customer or customers. It often can be visualized with a flowchart as a sequence of activities.

There are three types of _____ es:

1. Management processes, the processes that govern the operation of a system. Typical management processes include 'Corporate Governance' and 'Strategic Management'.
2. Operational processes, processes that constitute the core business and create the primary value stream. Typical operational processes are Purchasing, Manufacturing, Marketing, and Sales.
3. Supporting processes, which support the core processes. Examples include Accounting, Recruitment, Technical support.

A _____ begins with a customer's need and ends with a customer's need fulfillment. Process oriented organizations break down the barriers of structural departments and try to avoid functional silos.

a. 1990 Clean Air Act
b. 28-hour day
c. 33 Strategies of War
d. Business process

6. _____ is a systematic approach to help any organization optimize its underlying processes to achieve more efficient results.

The organization may be a for-profit business, a non-profit organization, a government agency, or any other ongoing concern. Most _____ techniques were developed and refined in the manufacturing era, though many of the methodologies (like Six Sigma) have been successfully adapted to work in the predominantly service-based economy of today.

a. Fix it twice
b. Contingency theory
c. Micromanagement
d. Business process improvement

7. _____ is, in computer science and management, an approach aiming at improvements by means of elevating efficiency and effectiveness of the business process that exist within and across organizations. The key to _____ is for organizations to look at their business processes from a 'clean slate' perspective and determine how they can best construct these processes to improve how they conduct business. _____ Cycle.

_____ is also known as _____, Business Process Redesign, Business Transformation, or Business Process Change Management.

a. Product life cycle
b. Horizontal integration
c. Personal management interview
d. Business process reengineering

8. In probability theory, a probability distribution is called _____ if its cumulative distribution function is _____. This is equivalent to saying that for random variables X with the distribution in question, Pr[X = a] = 0 for all real numbers a, i.e.: the probability that X attains the value a is zero, for any number a. If the distribution of X is _____ then X is called a _____ random variable.

a. Decision tree pruning
b. Pay Band
c. Connectionist expert systems
d. Continuous

9. _____ is a management process whereby delivery (customer valued) processes are constantly evaluated and improved in the light of their efficiency, effectiveness and flexibility.

Some see it as a meta process for most management systems (Business Process Management, Quality Management, Project Management). Deming saw it as part of the 'system' whereby feedback from the process and customer were evaluated against organisational goals.

a. Sole proprietorship
b. First-mover advantage
c. Continuous Improvement Process
d. Critical Success Factor

Chapter 1. INTRODUCTION

10. _____ refers to the movement of cash into or out of a business or financial product. It is usually measured during a specified, finite period of time. Measurement of _____ can be used

- to determine a project's rate of return or value. The time of _____s into and out of projects are used as inputs in financial models such as internal rate of return, and net present value.
- to determine problems with a business's liquidity. Being profitable does not necessarily mean being liquid. A company can fail because of a shortage of cash, even while profitable.
- as an alternate measure of a business's profits when it is believed that accrual accounting concepts do not represent economic realities. For example, a company may be notionally profitable but generating little operational cash (as may be the case for a company that barters its products rather than selling for cash.) In such a case, the company may be deriving additional operating cash by issuing shares evaluating default risk, re-investment requirements, etc.

_____ is a generic term used differently depending on the context. It may be defined by users for their own purposes.

a. Gross profit
c. Sweat equity
b. Gross profit margin
d. Cash flow

11. _____ is the discipline of planning, organizing and managing resources to bring about the successful completion of specific project goals and objectives. It is often closely related to and sometimes conflated with Program management.

A project is a finite endeavor--having specific start and completion dates--undertaken to meet particular goals and objectives, usually to bring about beneficial change or added value.

a. Project management
c. Precedence diagram
b. Project engineer
d. Work package

12. In organizational development (OD), _____ is a series of actions taken by a Process Owner to identify, analyze and improve existing processes within an organization to meet new goals and objectives. These actions often follow a specific methodology or strategy to create successful results. A sampling of these are listed below.

a. Product innovation
c. Letter of resignation
b. Supervisory board
d. Process improvement

13. _____ is, in very basic words, a position a firm occupies against its competitors.

According to Michael Porter, the three methods for creating a sustainable _____ are through:

1. Cost leadership

2. Differentiation

3. Focus (economics)

a. 28-hour day
c. Theory Z
b. 1990 Clean Air Act
d. Competitive advantage

14. The _____ is a concept from business management that was first described and popularized by Michael Porter in his 1985 best-seller, Competitive Advantage: Creating and Sustaining Superior Performance.

A _____ is a chain of activities. Products pass through all activities of the chain in order and at each activity the product gains some value. The chain of activities gives the products more added value than the sum of added values of all activities. It is important not to mix the concept of the _____ with the costs occurring throughout the activities.

   a. Market development
   c. Mass marketing
   b. Customer relationship management
   d. Value chain

15. The _____, widely known as ISO , is an international-standard-setting body composed of representatives from various national standards organizations. Founded on 23 February 1947, the organization promulgates worldwide proprietary industrial and commercial standards. It is headquartered in Geneva, Switzerland.
   a. A Stake in the Outcome
   c. AAAI
   b. International Organization for Standardization
   d. A4e

16. _____ is subcontracting a process, such as product design or manufacturing, to a third-party company. The decision to outsource is often made in the interest of lowering cost or making better use of time and energy costs, redirecting or conserving energy directed at the competencies of a particular business, or to make more efficient use of land, labor, capital, (information) technology and resources. _____ became part of the business lexicon during the 1980s.
   a. Opinion leadership
   c. Operant conditioning
   b. Unemployment insurance
   d. Outsourcing

17. The _____ is a performance management tool for measuring whether the smaller-scale operational activities of a company are aligned with its larger-scale objectives in terms of vision and strategy.

By focusing not only on financial outcomes but also on the operational, marketing and developmental inputs to these, the _____ helps provide a more comprehensive view of a business, which in turn helps organizations act in their best long-term interests. This tool is also being used to address business response to climate change and greenhouse gas emissions.

   a. Management development
   c. Middle management
   b. Balanced scorecard
   d. Commercial management

18. In corporate finance, _____ or _____ is an estimate of true economic profit after making corrective adjustments to GAAP accounting, including deducting the opportunity cost of equity capital. _____ can be measured as Net Operating Profit After Taxes(or NOPAT) less the money cost of capital. _____ is similar in nature to that of calculating another financial performance measure - Residual Income , however, there are a few complexities involved with coming up with the elements for calculating _____ over RI such as the myriad adjustments that might be made to NOPAT before it is suitable for the formula below.
   a. A4e
   c. A Stake in the Outcome
   b. AAAI
   d. Economic value added

Chapter 1. INTRODUCTION

19. _____ is a Japanese philosophy that focuses on continuous improvement throughout all aspects of life. When applied to the workplace, _____ activities continually improve all functions of a business, from manufacturing to management and from the CEO to the assembly line workers. By improving standardized activities and processes, _____ aims to eliminate waste .

   a. Kaizen
   b. Cross-docking
   c. Psychological pricing
   d. Sensitivity analysis

20. _____ refers to the difference between the cost of materials purchased by a company plus the cost of the labor to assemble a product and the price at which the company sells the product. An example is the price of gasoline at the pump over the price of the oil in it. In national accounts used in macroeconomics, it refers to the contribution of the factors of production, i.e., land, labor, and capital goods, to raising the value of a product and corresponds to the incomes received by the owners of these factors.

   a. Value added
   b. Minimum wage
   c. Deregulation
   d. Rehn-Meidner Model

21. _____ is understood as a business unit within the overall corporate identity which is distinguishable from other business because it serves a defined external market where management can conduct strategic planning in relation to products and markets. When companies become really large, they are best thought of as being composed of a number of businesses (or _____s.)

In the broader domain of strategic management, the phrase '_____' came into use in the 1960s, largely as a result of General Electric's many units.

   a. Strategic business unit
   b. Switching cost
   c. Strategic group
   d. Strategic drift

22. _____ is a costing model that identifies activities in an organization and assigns the cost of each activity resource to all products and services according to the actual consumption by each: it assigns more indirect costs (overhead) into direct costs.

In this way an organization can establish the true cost of its individual products and services for the purposes of identifying and eliminating those which are unprofitable and lowering the prices of those which are overpriced.

In a business organization, the ABC methodology assigns an organization's resource costs through activities to the products and services provided to its customers.

   a. A4e
   b. Indirect costs
   c. A Stake in the Outcome
   d. Activity-based costing

23. _____ consists of the processes a company uses to track and organize its contacts with its current and prospective customers. _____ software is used to support these processes; information about customers and customer interactions can be entered, stored and accessed by employees in different company departments. Typical _____ goals are to improve services provided to customers, and to use customer contact information for targeted marketing.

a. Disruptive technology
b. Green marketing
c. Marketing plan
d. Customer relationship management

24. _____ is an increasingly broadening term with which an organization, or other human system describes the combination of traditionally administrative personnel functions with acquisition and application of skills, knowledge and experience, Employee Relations and resource planning at various levels. The field draws upon concepts developed in Industrial/Organizational Psychology and System Theory. _____ has at least two related interpretations depending on context. The original usage derives from political economy and economics, where it was traditionally called labor, one of four factors of production although this perspective is changing as a function of new and ongoing research into more strategic approaches at national levels. This first usage is used more in terms of '_____ development', and can go beyond just organizations to the level of nations . The more traditional usage within corporations and businesses refers to the individuals within a firm or agency, and to the portion of the organization that deals with hiring, firing, training, and other personnel issues, typically referred to as `_____ management'.

a. Bradford Factor
b. Human resource management
c. Progressive discipline
d. Human resources

25. _____ is an idea in the field of Organizational studies and management which describes the psychology, attitudes, experiences, beliefs and Values (personal and cultural values) of an organization. It has been defined as 'the specific collection of values and norms that are shared by people and groups in an organization and that control the way they interact with each other and with stakeholders outside the organization.'

This definition continues to explain organizational values also known as 'beliefs and ideas about what kinds of goals members of an organization should pursue and ideas about the appropriate kinds or standards of behavior organizational members should use to achieve these goals. From organizational values develop organizational norms, guidelines or expectations that prescribe appropriate kinds of behavior by employees in particular situations and control the behavior of organizational members towards one another.'

_____ is not the same as corporate culture.

a. Organizational effectiveness
b. Organizational development
c. Union shop
d. Organizational culture

26. _____ is an advertisement in which a particular product specifically mentions a competitor by name for the express purpose of showing why the competitor is inferior to the product naming it.

This should not be confused with parody advertisements, where a fictional product is being advertised for the purpose of poking fun at the particular advertisement, nor should it be confused with the use of a coined brand name for the purpose of comparing the product without actually naming an actual competitor. ('Wikipedia tastes better and is less filling than the Encyclopedia Galactica.')

In the 1980s, during what has been referred to as the cola wars, soft-drink manufacturer Pepsi ran a series of advertisements where people, caught on hidden camera, in a blind taste test, chose Pepsi over rival Coca-Cola.

a. 28-hour day
b. 33 Strategies of War
c. 1990 Clean Air Act
d. Comparative advertising

Chapter 1. INTRODUCTION

27. _____ is a business management strategy aimed at embedding awareness of quality in all organizational processes. _____ has been widely used in manufacturing, education, hospitals, call centers, government, and service industries, as well as NASA space and science programs.

As defined by the International Organization for Standardization (ISO):

> '_____ is a management approach for an organization, centered on quality, based on the participation of all its members and aiming at long-term success through customer satisfaction, and benefits to all members of the organization and to society.' ISO 8402:1994

One major aim is to reduce variation from every process so that greater consistency of effort is obtained. (Royse, D., Thyer, B., Padgett D., ' Logan T., 2006)

a. Quality management
b. 1990 Clean Air Act
c. 28-hour day
d. Total quality management

28. _____ is a structured approach to transitioning individuals, teams, and organizations from a current state to a desired future state. The current definition of _____ includes both organizational _____ processes and individual _____ models, which together are used to manage the people side of change.

A number of models are available for understanding the transitioning of individuals through the phases of _____ and strengthening organizational development initiative in both government and corporate sectors.

a. 33 Strategies of War
b. Change management
c. 1990 Clean Air Act
d. 28-hour day

29. _____ can be considered to have three main components: quality control, quality assurance and quality improvement. _____ is focused not only on product quality, but also the means to achieve it. _____ therefore uses quality assurance and control of processes as well as products to achieve more consistent quality.

a. 1990 Clean Air Act
b. Quality management
c. Total quality management
d. 28-hour day

30. A _____ is a type of bar chart that illustrates a project schedule. _____s illustrate the start and finish dates of the terminal elements and summary elements of a project. Terminal elements and summary elements comprise the work breakdown structure of the project.

a. Gantt chart
b. 28-hour day
c. 1990 Clean Air Act
d. 33 Strategies of War

31. _____ is the concept of how effective an organization is in achieving the outcomes the organization intends to produce. The idea of _____ is especially important for non-profit organizations as most people who donate money to non-profit organizations and charities are interested in knowing whether the organization is effective in accomplishing its goals.

An organization's effectiveness is also dependent on its communicative competence and ethics.

Chapter 1. INTRODUCTION

a. Organizational development
b. Informal organization
c. Organizational effectiveness
d. Organizational structure

32. The general definition of an _____ is an evaluation of a person, organization, system, process, project or product. _____s are performed to ascertain the validity and reliability of information; also to provide an assessment of a system's internal control. The goal of an _____ is to express an opinion on the person / organization/system (etc) in question, under evaluation based on work done on a test basis.

a. Internal control
b. Audit committee
c. A Stake in the Outcome
d. Audit

33. _____ is one of the managerial functions like planning, organizing, staffing and directing. It is an important function because it helps to check the errors and to take the corrective action so that deviation from standards are minimized and stated goals of the organization are achieved in desired manner. According to modern concepts, _____ is a foreseeing action whereas earlier concept of _____ was used only when errors were detected. _____ in management means setting standards, measuring actual performance and taking corrective action.

a. Decision tree pruning
b. Schedule of reinforcement
c. Turnover
d. Control

34. In engineering and manufacturing, _____ and quality engineering are used in developing systems to ensure products or services are designed and produced to meet or exceed customer requirements. Refer to the definition by Merriam-Webster for further information. These systems are often developed in conjunction with other business and engineering disciplines using a cross-functional approach.

a. Process capability
b. Single Minute Exchange of Die
c. Statistical process control
d. Quality control

35. _____ is an integrated communications-based process through which individuals and communities discover that existing and newly-identified needs and wants may be satisfied by the products and services of others.

_____ is defined by the American _____ Association as the activity, set of institutions, and processes for creating, communicating, delivering, and exchanging offerings that have value for customers, clients, partners, and society at large. The term developed from the original meaning which referred literally to going to market, as in shopping, or going to a market to buy or sell goods or services.

a. Marketing
b. Market development
c. Customer relationship management
d. Disruptive technology

36. A _____ is a professional in the field of project management. _____s can have the responsibility of the planning, execution, and closing of any project, typically relating to construction industry, architecture, computer networking, telecommunications or software development.

Many other fields in the production, design and service industries also have _____s.

a. Project manager
b. Project engineer
c. Work package
d. Project management

37. An _____ is an organization founded and funded by businesses that operate in a specific industry. An industry trade association participates in public relations activities such as advertising, education, political donations, lobbying and publishing, but its main focus is collaboration between companies, or standardization. Associations may offer other services, such as producing conferences, networking or charitable events or offering classes or educational materials.

   a. Industry trade group   b. AAAI

   c. A4e   d. A Stake in the Outcome

38. _____ describes the situation when output from (or information about the result of) an event or phenomenon in the past will influence the same event/phenomenon in the present or future. When an event is part of a chain of cause-and-effect that forms a circuit or loop, then the event is said to 'feed back' into itself.

_____ is also a synonym for:

- _____ signal; the information about the initial event that is the basis for subsequent modification of the event.
- _____ loop; the causal path that leads from the initial generation of the _____ signal to the subsequent modification of the event.

_____ is a mechanism, process or signal that is looped back to control a system within itself. Such a loop is called a _____ loop.

   a. Positive feedback   b. 1990 Clean Air Act

   c. Feedback loop   d. Feedback

Chapter 2. CORPORATE-GOVERNANCE BEST PRACTICES

1. The _____ is a politically conservative group of chief executive officers of major U.S. corporations formed to promote pro-business public policy.

The group was formed in 1972 through the merger of three existing organizations: the March Group, consisting of chief executive officers who met informally to consider public policy issues; the Construction Users Anti-Inflation Roundtable, a group devoted to containing construction costs; and the Labor Law Study Committee, largely made up of labor relations executives of major companies.

It 'strongly supported passage of the' No Child Left Behind Act of 2002, 'and is now actively working with states on implementation.' It has issued press releases, submitted editorials, given congressional testimony and distributed position ads.

- a. Process-based management
- b. National Association for the Advancement of Colored People
- c. Business Roundtable
- d. Headquarters

2. _____ is the set of processes, customs, policies, laws, and institutions affecting the way a corporation (or company) is directed, administered or controlled. _____ also includes the relationships among the many stakeholders involved and the goals for which the corporation is governed. The principal stakeholders are the shareholders/members, management, and the board of directors.
- a. Corporate Governance
- b. Flextime
- c. Guarantee
- d. No-FEAR Act

3. _____ are formal records of the financial activities of a business, person, or other entity. In British English, including United Kingdom company law, _____ are often referred to as accounts, although the term _____ is also used, particularly by accountants.

_____ provide an overview of a business or person's financial condition in both short and long term.

- a. 1990 Clean Air Act
- b. 33 Strategies of War
- c. 28-hour day
- d. Financial statements

4. _____ generally refers to a list of all planned expenses and revenues. It is a plan for saving and spending. A _____ is an important concept in microeconomics, which uses a _____ line to illustrate the trade-offs between two or more goods.
- a. 28-hour day
- b. Budget
- c. 33 Strategies of War
- d. 1990 Clean Air Act

5. The general definition of an _____ is an evaluation of a person, organization, system, process, project or product. _____s are performed to ascertain the validity and reliability of information; also to provide an assessment of a system's internal control. The goal of an _____ is to express an opinion on the person / organization/system (etc) in question, under evaluation based on work done on a test basis.
- a. Internal control
- b. A Stake in the Outcome
- c. Audit committee
- d. Audit

Chapter 2. CORPORATE-GOVERNANCE BEST PRACTICES

6. In a publicly-held company, an _____ is an operating committee of the Board of Directors, typically charged with oversight of financial reporting and disclosure. Committee members are drawn from members of the Company's board of directors, with a Chairperson selected from among the members. An _____ of a publicly-traded company in the United States is composed of independent and outside directors referred to as non-executive directors, at least one of which is typically a financial expert.
   a. A Stake in the Outcome
   b. Internal auditing
   c. Internal control
   d. Audit committee

7. _____ is a structured approach to transitioning individuals, teams, and organizations from a current state to a desired future state. The current definition of _____ includes both organizational _____ processes and individual _____ models, which together are used to manage the people side of change.

A number of models are available for understanding the transitioning of individuals through the phases of _____ and strengthening organizational development initiative in both government and corporate sectors.

   a. 28-hour day
   b. 33 Strategies of War
   c. 1990 Clean Air Act
   d. Change management

8. A _____ is responsible for administrative management of private, public or governmental corporations. The _____ is one of the highest ranking members of an organization, managing daily operations and usually reporting directly to the chief executive officer. In some companies, the _____ is also the president.
   a. Chief knowledge officer
   b. Chief technology officer
   c. Hotel manager
   d. Chief administrative officer

9. A _____ or chief executive is one of the highest-ranking corporate officer (executive) or administrator in charge of total management. An individual selected as President and _____ of a corporation, company, organization, or agency, reports to the board of directors. In internal communication and press releases, many companies capitalize the term and those of other high positions, even when they are not proper nouns.
   a. Purchasing manager
   b. Chief brand officer
   c. Financial analyst
   d. Chief executive officer

10. The _____ of a company or public agency is the corporate officer primarily responsible for managing the financial risks of the business or agency. This officer is also responsible for financial planning and record-keeping, as well as financial reporting to higher management. (In recent years, however, the role has expanded to encompass communicating financial performance and forecasts to the analyst community.)
    a. Chief financial officer
    b. 33 Strategies of War
    c. 1990 Clean Air Act
    d. 28-hour day

11. Chief Governing Officer or _____. Defined term in some municipalities, organizations, or corporations as the alternative or secondary title for a Chairman of the Board (also Chairman, Chairperson, Chairwoman, Chair), especially in entities that generally have a separation of powers between the Chairman and the Chief Executive Officer (CEO), generally denoting supervision by the _____, as head of the board and supervisor of the President and/or the CEO, etc.
    a. Chief governance officer
    b. Dual board
    c. Shareholder resolutions
    d. Standing proxy

Chapter 2. CORPORATE-GOVERNANCE BEST PRACTICES

12. The _____ is a job title for the board level head of information technology within an organization. The _____ typically reports to the chief operations officer or the chief executive officer. In military organizations, they report to the commanding officer or commanding general of the organization.

a. 28-hour day
b. 33 Strategies of War
c. 1990 Clean Air Act
d. Chief information officer

13. A _____ is the highest-ranking corporate officer concerning legal affairs of a corporation or agency. _____s typically hold the title of general counsel.

_____s are attorneys, but their skill level should not be limited to the law.

a. Value based pricing
b. Centralization
c. Product innovation
d. Chief legal officer

14. _____ is a corporate title referring to an executive responsible for various marketing in an organization. Most often the position reports to the chief executive officer.

With primary or shared responsibility for areas such as sales management, product development, distribution channel management, public relations, marketing communications (including advertising and promotions), pricing, market research, and customer service, _____s are faced with a diverse range of specialized disciplines in which they are forced to be knowledgeable.

a. Chief marketing officer
b. Business Roundtable
c. Food Marketing Institute
d. Small and medium enterprises

15. A _____ or chief operations officer is a corporate officer responsible for managing the day-to-day activities of the corporation and for operations management (OM.) The _____ is one of the highest-ranking members of an organization's senior management, monitoring the daily operations of the company and reporting to the board of directors and the top executive officer, usually the chief executive officer (CEO.) The _____ is usually an executive or senior officer.

a. Product innovation
b. Chief operating officer
c. Value based pricing
d. Supervisory board

16. _____ is an advertisement in which a particular product specifically mentions a competitor by name for the express purpose of showing why the competitor is inferior to the product naming it.

This should not be confused with parody advertisements, where a fictional product is being advertised for the purpose of poking fun at the particular advertisement, nor should it be confused with the use of a coined brand name for the purpose of comparing the product without actually naming an actual competitor. ('Wikipedia tastes better and is less filling than the Encyclopedia Galactica.')

In the 1980s, during what has been referred to as the cola wars, soft-drink manufacturer Pepsi ran a series of advertisements where people, caught on hidden camera, in a blind taste test, chose Pepsi over rival Coca-Cola.

a. 1990 Clean Air Act
b. 28-hour day
c. Comparative advertising
d. 33 Strategies of War

Chapter 2. CORPORATE-GOVERNANCE BEST PRACTICES

17. While _____ literally refers to a person responsible for the performance of duties involved in running an organization, the exact meaning of the role is variable, depending on the organization.

While there is no clear line between executive or principal and inferior officers, principal officers are high-level officials in the executive branch of U.S. government such as department heads of independent agencies. In Humphrey's Executor v. United States, 295 U.S. 602 (1935), the Court distinguished between _____s and quasi-legislative or quasi-judicial officers by stating that the former serve at the pleasure of the President and may be removed at his discretion.

   a. Executive officer   b. Australian Fair Pay and Conditions Standard
   c. Easement   d. Unreported employment

18. _____ is an integrated communications-based process through which individuals and communities discover that existing and newly-identified needs and wants may be satisfied by the products and services of others.

_____ is defined by the American _____ Association as the activity, set of institutions, and processes for creating, communicating, delivering, and exchanging offerings that have value for customers, clients, partners, and society at large. The term developed from the original meaning which referred literally to going to market, as in shopping, or going to a market to buy or sell goods or services.

   a. Market development   b. Disruptive technology
   c. Marketing   d. Customer relationship management

19. The phrase _____, according to the Organization for Economic Co-operation and Development, refers to 'creative work undertaken on a systematic basis in order to increase the stock of knowledge, including knowledge of man, culture and society, and the use of this stock of knowledge to devise new applications [sic]'

New product design and development is more than often a crucial factor in the survival of a company. In an industry that is fast changing, firms must continually revise their design and range of products. This is necessary due to continuous technology change and development as well as other competitors and the changing preference of customers.

   a. 28-hour day   b. 1990 Clean Air Act
   c. 33 Strategies of War   d. Research and development

20. A _____ is a body of elected or appointed members who jointly oversee the activities of a company or organization. The body sometimes has a different name, such as board of trustees, board of governors, board of managers, or executive board. It is often simply referred to as 'the board.'

A board's activities are determined by the powers, duties, and responsibilities delegated to it or conferred on it by an authority outside itself.

   a. Clean Water Act   b. Competition law
   c. Foreign Corrupt Practices Act   d. Board of directors

Chapter 2. CORPORATE-GOVERNANCE BEST PRACTICES

21. The _____ or chief risk management officer (CRMO) of a corporation is the executive accountable for enabling the efficient and effective governance of significant risks, and related opportunities, to a business and its various segments. Risks are commonly categorized as strategic, reputational, operational, financial, or compliance-related. _____'s are accountable to the Executive Committee and The Board for enabling the business to balance risk and reward.
   a. Headquarters
   b. Boundaryless organization
   c. Person Analysis
   d. Chief risk officer

22. A _____ is an executive position whose holder is focused on scientific and technical issues within an organization. Essentially, a _____ is responsible for the transformation of capital - be it monetary, intellectual, or political - into technology in furtherance of the company's objectives.

   The title is most typically found in organizations which significantly develop or exploit information technology.

   a. Managing director
   b. Chief technology officer
   c. General Manager
   d. Chief knowledge officer

23. _____ is an increasingly broadening term with which an organization, or other human system describes the combination of traditionally administrative personnel functions with acquisition and application of skills, knowledge and experience, Employee Relations and resource planning at various levels. The field draws upon concepts developed in Industrial/Organizational Psychology and System Theory. _____ has at least two related interpretations depending on context. The original usage derives from political economy and economics, where it was traditionally called labor, one of four factors of production although this perspective is changing as a function of new and ongoing research into more strategic approaches at national levels. This first usage is used more in terms of '_____ development', and can go beyond just organizations to the level of nations. The more traditional usage within corporations and businesses refers to the individuals within a firm or agency, and to the portion of the organization that deals with hiring, firing, training, and other personnel issues, typically referred to as '_____ management'.
   a. Bradford Factor
   b. Progressive discipline
   c. Human resource management
   d. Human resources

24. _____ is the acquisition of goods and/or services at the best possible total cost of ownership, in the right quality and quantity, at the right time, in the right place and from the right source for the direct benefit or use of corporations, individuals generally via a contract. Simple _____ may involve nothing more than repeat purchasing. Complex _____ could involve finding long term partners - or even 'co-destiny' suppliers that might fundamentally commit one organization to another.
   a. Golden parachute
   b. Sole proprietorship
   c. Psychological pricing
   d. Procurement

25. In decision theory and estimation theory, the _____ of an estimator, $\hat{\theta}$, of an unknown parameter of the distribution, θ, is the expected value of the loss function

$$R(\theta, \hat{\theta}) = \mathbb{E}_\theta L(\theta, \hat{\theta}) = \int L(\theta, \hat{\theta})\, dP_\theta.$$

where dP_θ is a probability measure parametrized by θ.

- For a scalar parameter θ and a quadratic loss function,

$$L(\theta, \hat{\theta}) = (\theta - \hat{\theta})^2$$

  the _____ function becomes the mean squared error of the estimate,

$$R(\theta, \hat{\theta}) = E_\theta (\theta - \hat{\theta})^2$$

- In density estimation, the unknown parameter is probability density itself. The loss function is typically chosen to be a norm in an appropriate function space. For example, for L^2 norm,

$$L(f, \hat{f}) = \|f - \hat{f}\|_2^2$$

  the _____ function becomes the mean integrated squared error

$$R(f, \hat{f}) = E\|f - \hat{f}\|^2$$

a. Risk aversion
b. Linear model
c. Financial modeling
d. Risk

26. _____ is the identification, assessment, and prioritization of risks followed by coordinated and economical application of resources to minimize, monitor, and control the probability and/or impact of unfortunate events.. Risks can come from uncertainty in financial markets, project failures, legal liabilities, credit risk, accidents, natural causes and disasters as well as deliberate attacks from an adversary. Several _____ standards have been developed including the Project Management Institute, the National Institute of Science and Technology, actuarial societies, and ISO standards.
  a. Kanban
  b. Succession planning
  c. Trademark
  d. Risk management

27. A _____ is the belief that there is a technique, method, process, activity, incentive or reward that is more effective at delivering a particular outcome than any other technique, method, process, etc. The idea is that with proper processes, checks, and testing, a desired outcome can be delivered with fewer problems and unforeseen complications. _____s can also be defined as the most efficient (least amount of effort) and effective (best results) way of accomplishing a task, based on repeatable procedures that have proven themselves over time for large numbers of people.
  a. Fix it twice
  b. Hierarchical organization
  c. Design management
  d. Best practice

28. _____ in its literal sense is the process of transformation of local or regional phenomena into global ones. It can be described as a process by which the people of the world are unified into a single society and function together.

Chapter 2. CORPORATE-GOVERNANCE BEST PRACTICES

This process is a combination of economic, technological, sociocultural and political forces.

a. Globalization
b. Cost Management
c. Collaborative Planning, Forecasting and Replenishment
d. Histogram

29. The _____ captures an expanded spectrum of values and criteria for measuring organizational success: economic, ecological and social. With the ratification of the United Nations and ICLEI _____ standard for urban and community accounting in early 2007, this became the dominant approach to public sector full cost accounting. Similar UN standards apply to natural capital and human capital measurement to assist in measurements required by _____, e.g. the ecoBudget standard for reporting ecological footprint.

a. Triple bottom line
b. 33 Strategies of War
c. 1990 Clean Air Act
d. 28-hour day

30. _____ is a term used in corporate law to describe a fiduciaries' 'conflicts of interest and requires fiduciaries to put the corporation's interests ahead of their own.' 'Corporate fiduciaries breach their _____ when they divert corporate assets, opportunities, or information for personal gain.'

It is generally acceptable if a director makes a decision for the corporation that profits both him and the corporation. The _____ is breached when the director puts their interest in front of that of the corporation.

- Flagrant Diversion: corporate official stealing tangible corporate assets - 'a plain breach of the fiduciary's _____ since the diversion was unauthorized and the corporation received no benefit in the transaction.'
- Self-Dealing: A key player and the corporation are on opposite sides of the transaction or the key player has helped influence the corporation's decisions to enter the transaction. 'When a fiduciary enters into a transaction with the corporation on unfair terms, the effect is the same as if he had appropriated the difference between the transaction's fair value and the transaction's price.'
- Executive Compensation
- Usurping Corporate Opportunity
- Disclosure to Shareholders
- Trading on Inside Information
- Selling out
- Entrenchment
- The key player's personal financial interest are at least potentially in conflict with the financial interests of the corporation.

- By showing approval by a majority of disinterested directors
- Showing ratification by shareholders (MBCA 8.63)
- Showing transaction was inherently fair (MBCA 8.61)

Section 8.60 of the Model Business Corporation Act states there is a conflict of interest when the director knows that at the time of a commitment that he or a related person is 1) a party to the transaction or 2) has a beneficial financial interest in the transaction that the interest and exercises his influence to the detriment of the corporation.

a. Clayton Antitrust Act
b. Competition law
c. Corporate governance
d. Duty of loyalty

31. _____ is a concept in ethics with several meanings. It is often used synonymously with such concepts as responsibility, answerability, enforcement, blameworthiness, liability and other terms associated with the expectation of account-giving. As an aspect of governance, it has been central to discussions related to problems in both the public and private (corporation) worlds.
  a. Usury
  b. A4e
  c. A Stake in the Outcome
  d. Accountability

32. In accounting and auditing, _____ is defined as a process effected by an organization's structure, work and authority flows, people and management information systems, designed to help the organization accomplish specific goals or objectives. It is a means by which an organization's resources are directed, monitored, and measured. It plays an important role in preventing and detecting fraud and protecting the organization's resources, both physical (e.g., machinery and property) and intangible (e.g., reputation or intellectual property such as trademarks.)
  a. Audit committee
  b. Internal auditing
  c. A Stake in the Outcome
  d. Internal control

33. _____ is one of the managerial functions like planning, organizing, staffing and directing. It is an important function because it helps to check the errors and to take the corrective action so that deviation from standards are minimized and stated goals of the organization are achieved in desired manner. According to modern concepts, _____ is a foreseeing action whereas earlier concept of _____ was used only when errors were detected. _____ in management means setting standards, measuring actual performance and taking corrective action.
  a. Schedule of reinforcement
  b. Turnover
  c. Control
  d. Decision tree pruning

34. A _____ is a list of the general tasks and responsibilities of a position. Typically, it also includes to whom the position reports, specifications such as the qualifications needed by the person in the job, salary range for the position, etc. A _____ is usually developed by conducting a job analysis, which includes examining the tasks and sequences of tasks necessary to perform the job.
  a. Recruitment
  b. Recruitment Process Insourcing
  c. Recruitment advertising
  d. Job description

35. A _____ occurs when an individual or organization (such as a policeman, lawyer, insurance adjuster, politician, engineer, executive, director of a corporation, medical research scientist, physician, writer, editor, or any other entrusted individual or organization) has an interest that might compromise their actions. The presence of a _____ is independent from the execution of impropriety.

In the legal profession, the duty of loyalty owed to a client prohibits an attorney (or a law firm) from representing any other party with interests adverse to those of a current client.

  a. 1990 Clean Air Act
  b. 28-hour day
  c. Conflict of interest
  d. Global Corruption Report

Chapter 2. CORPORATE-GOVERNANCE BEST PRACTICES

36. The _____ is an independent, not-for-profit membership organization, dedicated to serving the corporate governance needs of directors of public, private, and non-profit organizations. Founded in 1977, NACD is headquartered in Washington, D.C. and serves approximately 10,000 members. NACD's stated mission is to achieve improved corporate performance through better board practice.

   a. Financial Accounting Standards Board
   b. Business Roundtable
   c. Goodyear Tire ' Rubber
   d. National Association of Corporate Directors

37. _____ is an organization's process of defining its strategy and making decisions on allocating its resources to pursue this strategy, including its capital and people. Various business analysis techniques can be used in _____, including SWOT analysis (Strengths, Weaknesses, Opportunities, and Threats) and PEST analysis (Political, Economic, Social, and Technological analysis) or STEER analysis involving Socio-cultural, Technological, Economic, Ecological, and Regulatory factors and EPISTEL (Environment, Political, Informatic, Social, Technological, Economic and Legal)

_____ is the formal consideration of an organization's future course. All _____ deals with at least one of three key questions:

   1. 'What do we do?'
   2. 'For whom do we do it?'
   3. 'How do we excel?'

In business _____, the third question is better phrased 'How can we beat or avoid competition?'. (Bradford and Duncan, page 1.)

   a. 1990 Clean Air Act
   b. 28-hour day
   c. 33 Strategies of War
   d. Strategic planning

38. In probability theory, a probability distribution is called _____ if its cumulative distribution function is _____. This is equivalent to saying that for random variables X with the distribution in question, Pr[X = a] = 0 for all real numbers a, i.e.: the probability that X attains the value a is zero, for any number a. If the distribution of X is _____ then X is called a _____ random variable.

   a. Decision tree pruning
   b. Pay Band
   c. Connectionist expert systems
   d. Continuous

39. _____ is a management process whereby delivery (customer valued) processes are constantly evaluated and improved in the light of their efficiency, effectiveness and flexibility.

Some see it as a meta process for most management systems (Business Process Management, Quality Management, Project Management). Deming saw it as part of the 'system' whereby feedback from the process and customer were evaluated against organisational goals.

   a. Continuous Improvement Process
   b. Critical Success Factor
   c. First-mover advantage
   d. Sole proprietorship

40. _____ is the process by which an organization deals with any major unpredictable event that threatens to harm the organization, its stakeholders, or the general public. Three elements are common to most definitions of crisis: (a) a threat to the organization, (b) the element of surprise, and (c) a short decision time.

Whereas risk management involves assessing potential threats and finding the best ways to avoid those threats, _____ involves dealing with the disasters after they have occurred.

a. C-A-K-E
b. Business value
c. Capability management
d. Crisis management

41. A _____ is defined as someone who controls access to something. It also refers to individuals who decide whether a given message will be distributed by a mass medium.

_____s serve several different purposes such as academic admissions, financial advising, and news editing.

a. 28-hour day
b. 1990 Clean Air Act
c. 33 Strategies of War
d. Gatekeeper

42. _____ is the planning process used to determine whether a firm's long term investments such as new machinery, replacement machinery, new plants, new products, and research development projects are worth pursuing. It is budget for major capital, or investment, expenditures.

Many formal methods are used in _____, including the techniques such as

- Net present value
- Profitability index
- Internal rate of return
- Modified Internal Rate of Return
- Equivalent annuity

These methods use the incremental cash flows from each potential investment, or project. Techniques based on accounting earnings and accounting rules are sometimes used - though economists consider this to be improper - such as the accounting rate of return, and 'return on investment.' Simplified and hybrid methods are used as well, such as payback period and discounted payback period.

a. Gross profit
b. Restricted stock
c. Gross profit margin
d. Capital budgeting

43. _____ and benefits in kind are various non-wage compensations provided to employees in addition to their normal wages or salaries. Where an employee exchanges (cash) wages for some other form of benefit, this is generally referred to as a 'salary sacrifice' arrangement. In most countries, most kinds of _____ are taxable to at least some degree.

a. A4e
b. Interactive Accommodation Process
c. A Stake in the Outcome
d. Employee benefits

Chapter 2. CORPORATE-GOVERNANCE BEST PRACTICES

44. The _____, first published in 1952, is one of a number of uniform acts that have been promulgated in conjunction with efforts to harmonize the law of sales and other commercial transactions in all 50 states within the United States of America. This objective is deemed important because of the prevalence of commercial transactions that extend beyond one state (for example, where the goods are manufactured in state A, warehoused in state B, sold from state C and delivered in state D.) The _____ deals primarily with transactions involving personal property (movable property), not real property (immovable property.)

a. AAAI
b. Uniform Commercial Code
c. A4e
d. A Stake in the Outcome

45. The _____ of 2002 (Pub.L. 107-204, 116 Stat. 745, enacted July 30, 2002), also known as the Public Company Accounting Reform and Investor Protection Act of 2002 and commonly called Sarbanes-Oxley, Sarbox or SOX, is a United States federal law enacted on July 30, 2002, as a reaction to a number of major corporate and accounting scandals including those affecting Enron, Tyco International, Adelphia, Peregrine Systems and WorldCom.

a. Sarbanes-Oxley Act
b. Fair Labor Standards Act
c. Sarbanes-Oxley Act of 2002
d. Letter of credit

46. _____ is a step in a risk management process. _____ is the determination of quantitative or qualitative value of risk related to a concrete situation and a recognized threat (also called hazard.) Quantitative _____ requires calculations of two components of risk: R, the magnitude of the potential loss L, and the probability p, that the loss will occur.

a. Quality assurance
b. 28-hour day
c. Risk assessment
d. 1990 Clean Air Act

47. _____ is the provision of service to customers before, during and after a purchase.

According to Turban et al. (2002), '_____ is a series of activities designed to enhance the level of customer satisfaction - that is, the feeling that a product or service has met the customer expectation.'

Its importance varies by product, industry and customer; defective or broken merchandise can be exchanged, often only with a receipt and within a specified time frame.

a. Customer service
b. 28-hour day
c. Service rate
d. 1990 Clean Air Act

48. _____ is the process of comparing the cost, cycle time, productivity, or quality of a specific process or method to another that is widely considered to be an industry standard or best practice. Essentially, _____ provides a snapshot of the performance of your business and helps you understand where you are in relation to a particular standard. The result is often a business case for making changes in order to make improvements.

a. Complementors
b. Competitive heterogeneity
c. Cost leadership
d. Benchmarking

49. A _____ is the highest-ranking corporate officer concerning talent or learning management of a corporation or agency. _____s can be experts in corporate or personal training, with degrees in education, instructional design or similar.

Qualified _____s of corporations should have leadership skills and be able clearly handle the training management of their company.

Chapter 2. CORPORATE-GOVERNANCE BEST PRACTICES 21

a. Cadbury Report
b. King I
c. Chief learning officer
d. Corporate headquarters

50. _____ refers to the stock of skills and knowledge embodied in the ability to perform labor so as to produce economic value. It is the skills and knowledge gained by a worker through education and experience. Many early economic theories refer to it simply as labor, one of three factors of production, and consider it to be a fungible resource -- homogeneous and easily interchangeable.

a. Market structure
b. Human capital
c. Deflation
d. Productivity management

51. _____ is normally any risk associated with any form of financing. Risk is probability of unfavorable condition; in financial sector it is the probability of actual return being less than expected return. There will be uncertainty in every business; the level of uncertainty present is called risk.

a. Choquet integral
b. Long term investment plan
c. Holding cost
d. Financial risk

52. The _____, widely known as ISO , is an international-standard-setting body composed of representatives from various national standards organizations. Founded on 23 February 1947, the organization promulgates worldwide proprietary industrial and commercial standards. It is headquartered in Geneva, Switzerland.

a. A Stake in the Outcome
b. A4e
c. AAAI
d. International Organization for Standardization

53. _____ is a business management strategy, initially implemented by Motorola, that today enjoys widespread application in many sectors of industry.

_____ seeks to improve the quality of process outputs by identifying and removing the causes of defects (errors) and variation in manufacturing and business processes. It uses a set of quality management methods, including statistical methods, and creates a special infrastructure of people within the organization ('Black Belts' etc.)

a. Takt time
b. Six Sigma
c. Theory of constraints
d. Production line

54. A _____ or business method is a collection of related, structured activities or tasks that produce a specific service or product (serve a particular goal) for a particular customer or customers. It often can be visualized with a flowchart as a sequence of activities.

There are three types of _____es:

1. Management processes, the processes that govern the operation of a system. Typical management processes include 'Corporate Governance' and 'Strategic Management'.
2. Operational processes, processes that constitute the core business and create the primary value stream. Typical operational processes are Purchasing, Manufacturing, Marketing, and Sales.
3. Supporting processes, which support the core processes. Examples include Accounting, Recruitment, Technical support.

A _____ begins with a customer's need and ends with a customer's need fulfillment. Process oriented organizations break down the barriers of structural departments and try to avoid functional silos.

a. 1990 Clean Air Act
b. Business process
c. 33 Strategies of War
d. 28-hour day

55. A _____ is a formula, practice, process, design, instrument, pattern by which a business can obtain an economic advantage over competitors or customers. In some jurisdictions, such secrets are referred to as 'confidential information' or 'classified information'.

The precise language by which a _____ is defined varies by jurisdiction (as do the particular types of information that are subject to _____ protection.)

a. Business valuation
b. Trade secret
c. Federal Trade Commission Act
d. Right to Financial Privacy Act

56. _____. The objective of OD is to improve the organization's capacity to handle its internal and external functioning and relationships. This would include such things as improved interpersonal and group processes, more effective communication, enhanced ability to cope with organizational problems of all kinds, more effective decision processes, more appropriate leadership style, improved skill in dealing with destructive conflict, and higher levels of trust and cooperation among organizational members.

a. Organizational development
b. Organizational structure
c. Industrial relations
d. Improved Organizational Performance

57. _____ is a 'method to transform user demands into design quality, to deploy the functions forming quality, and to deploy methods for achieving the design quality into subsystems and component parts, and ultimately to specific elements of the manufacturing process.', as described by Dr. Yoji Akao, who originally developed _____ in Japan in 1966, when the author combined his work in quality assurance and quality control points with function deployment used in Value Engineering.

_____ is designed to help planners focus on characteristics of a new or existing product or service from the viewpoints of market segments, company, or technology-development needs. The technique yields graphs and matrices.

a. Hoshin Kanri
b. Learning organization
c. 1990 Clean Air Act
d. Quality function deployment

58. _____ is a term used in business and Information Technology (through ITIL) to describe the process of capturing a customer's requirements. Specifically, the _____ is a market research technique that produces a detailed set of customer wants and needs, organized into a hierarchical structure, and then prioritized in terms of relative importance and satisfaction with current alternatives. _____ studies typically consist of both qualitative and quantitative research steps.

a. Goal setting
b. Board of governors
c. Business philosophy
d. Voice of the customer

Chapter 2. CORPORATE-GOVERNANCE BEST PRACTICES

59. _____ is a term that refers both to:

- a formal discipline used to help appraise, or assess, the case for a project or proposal, which itself is a process known as project appraisal; and
- an informal approach to making decisions of any kind.

Under both definitions the process involves, whether explicitly or implicitly, weighing the total expected costs against the total expected benefits of one or more actions in order to choose the best or most profitable option. The formal process is often referred to as either CBA (_____) or BCost-benefit analysis

A hallmark of CBA is that all benefits and all costs are expressed in money terms, and are adjusted for the time value of money, so that all flows of benefits and flows of project costs over time (which tend to occur at different points in time) are expressed on a common basis in terms of their 'present value.' Closely related, but slightly different, formal techniques include Cost-effectiveness analysis, Economic impact analysis, Fiscal impact analysis and Social Return on Investment(SROI) analysis. The latter builds upon the logic of _____, but differs in that it is explicitly designed to inform the practical decision-making of enterprise managers and investors focused on optimising their social and environmental impacts.

a. Decision engineering
b. Gittins index
c. Kepner-Tregoe
d. Cost-benefit analysis

60. In business and economics, _____ is a business resource assessment tool enabling a company to compare its actual performance with its potential performance. At its core are two questions: 'Where are we?' and 'Where do we want to be?' If a company or organization is under-utilizing its current resources or is forgoing investment in capital or technology, then it may be producing or performing at a level below its potential. This concept is similar to the base case of being below one's production possibilities frontier.

a. Cross-selling
b. Yield management
c. Business networking
d. Gap analysis

61. _____ is the term used to refer to the standard framework of guidelines for financial accounting used in any given jurisdiction. _____ includes the standards, conventions, and rules accountants follow in recording and summarizing transactions, and in the preparation of financial statements.

Financial accounting is information that must be assembled and reported objectively.

a. Net income
b. Treasury stock
c. Depreciation
d. Generally accepted accounting principles

Chapter 2. CORPORATE-GOVERNANCE BEST PRACTICES

62. _____ refers to the movement of cash into or out of a business or financial product. It is usually measured during a specified, finite period of time. Measurement of _____ can be used

- to determine a project's rate of return or value. The time of _____s into and out of projects are used as inputs in financial models such as internal rate of return, and net present value.
- to determine problems with a business's liquidity. Being profitable does not necessarily mean being liquid. A company can fail because of a shortage of cash, even while profitable.
- as an alternate measure of a business's profits when it is believed that accrual accounting concepts do not represent economic realities. For example, a company may be notionally profitable but generating little operational cash (as may be the case for a company that barters its products rather than selling for cash.) In such a case, the company may be deriving additional operating cash by issuing shares evaluating default risk, re-investment requirements, etc.

_____ is a generic term used differently depending on the context. It may be defined by users for their own purposes.

a. Gross profit
c. Sweat equity
b. Cash flow
d. Gross profit margin

63. _____ is the discipline of planning, organizing and managing resources to bring about the successful completion of specific project goals and objectives. It is often closely related to and sometimes conflated with Program management.

A project is a finite endeavor--having specific start and completion dates--undertaken to meet particular goals and objectives, usually to bring about beneficial change or added value.

a. Project management
c. Precedence diagram
b. Project engineer
d. Work package

64. _____ is a strategic planning method used to evaluate the Strengths, Weaknesses, Opportunities, and Threats involved in a project or in a business venture. It involves specifying the objective of the business venture or project and identifying the internal and external factors that are favorable and unfavorable to achieving that objective. The technique is credited to Albert Humphrey, who led a convention at Stanford University in the 1960s and 1970s using data from Fortune 500 companies.

a. Marketing
c. Corporate image
b. SWOT analysis
d. Market share

65. A _____ in project management and systems engineering, is a tool used to define and group a project's discrete work elements (or tasks) in a way that helps organize and define the total work scope of the project.

A _____ element may be a product, data, a service, or any combination. A _____ also provides the necessary framework for detailed cost estimating and control along with providing guidance for schedule development and control.

a. 1990 Clean Air Act
c. 33 Strategies of War
b. 28-hour day
d. Work breakdown structure

Chapter 2. CORPORATE-GOVERNANCE BEST PRACTICES

66. The _____, is a mathematically based algorithm for scheduling a set of project activities. It is an important tool for effective project management.

It was developed in the 1950s by the Dupont Corporation at about the same time that General Dynamics and the US Navy were developing the Program Evaluation and Review Technique (PERT) Today, it is commonly used with all forms of projects, including construction, software development, research projects, product development, engineering, and plant maintenance, among others.

   a. 28-hour day
   c. 33 Strategies of War
   b. 1990 Clean Air Act
   d. Critical path method

67. _____ is subcontracting a process, such as product design or manufacturing, to a third-party company. The decision to outsource is often made in the interest of lowering cost or making better use of time and energy costs, redirecting or conserving energy directed at the competencies of a particular business, or to make more efficient use of land, labor, capital, (information) technology and resources. _____ became part of the business lexicon during the 1980s.
   a. Opinion leadership
   c. Operant conditioning
   b. Unemployment insurance
   d. Outsourcing

68. The Program (or Project) Evaluation and Review Technique, commonly abbreviated _____, is a model for project management designed to analyze and represent the tasks involved in completing a given project.

_____ is a method to analyze the involved tasks in completing a given project, specially the time needed to complete each task, and identifying the minimum time needed to complete the total project.

_____ was developed primarily to simplify the planning and scheduling of large and complex projects.

   a. 33 Strategies of War
   c. 28-hour day
   b. 1990 Clean Air Act
   d. PERT

69. _____ describes the goal that corporations or public agencies aspire to in their efforts to ensure that personnel are aware of and take steps to comply with relevant laws and regulations.

The International Organisation for Standardisation (ISO) produces international standards such as ISO17799. The International Electrotechnical Commission (IEC) produces international standards in the electrotechnology area.

   a. Civil Rights Act of 1991
   c. Social Security Act of 1965
   b. Regulatory compliance
   d. Copyright Act of 1976

70. The _____ is an Act of the 106th United States Congress which repealed part of the Glass-Steagall Act of 1933, opening up competition among banks, securities companies and insurance companies.
   a. Gramm-Leach-Bliley Act
   c. 1990 Clean Air Act
   b. 33 Strategies of War
   d. 28-hour day

Chapter 2. CORPORATE-GOVERNANCE BEST PRACTICES

71. A _____ is a set of instructions having the force of a directive, covering those features of operations that lend themselves to a definite or standardized procedure without loss of effectiveness. Standard Operating Policies and Procedures can be effective catalysts to drive performance improvement and improving organizational results.
   a. Risk-benefit analysis
   b. Longitudinal study
   c. 1990 Clean Air Act
   d. Standard operating procedure

72. _____ is a cross-disciplinary area concerned with protecting the safety, health and welfare of people engaged in work or employment. The goal of all _____ programs is to foster a work free safe environment. As a secondary effect, it may also protect co-workers, family members, employers, customers, suppliers, nearby communities, and other members of the public who are impacted by the workplace environment.
   a. AAAI
   b. A Stake in the Outcome
   c. A4e
   d. Occupational Safety and Health

73. The _____ is the primary federal law which governs occupational health and safety in the private sector and federal government in the United States. It was enacted by Congress in 1970 and was signed by President Richard Nixon on December 29, 1970. Its main goal is to ensure that employers provide employees with an environment free from recognized hazards, such as exposure to toxic chemicals, excessive noise levels, mechanical dangers, heat or cold stress, or unsanitary conditions.
   a. Unemployment and Farm Relief Act
   b. Occupational Safety and Health Act
   c. Unemployment Action Center
   d. United States Department of Justice

74. In probability theory and statistics, the _____ of a random variable is the integral of the random variable with respect to its probability measure. For discrete random variables this is equivalent to the probability-weighted sum of the possible values, and for continuous random variables with a density function it is the probability density -weighted integral of the possible values.
   a. A4e
   b. AAAI
   c. Expected value
   d. A Stake in the Outcome

75. _____ is the study of how the variation (uncertainty) in the output of a mathematical model can be apportioned, qualitatively or quantitatively, to different sources of variation in the input of a model .

In more general terms uncertainty and sensitivity analyses investigate the robustness of a study when the study includes some form of mathematical modelling. While uncertainty analysis studies the overall uncertainty in the conclusions of the study, _____ tries to identify what source of uncertainty weights more on the study's conclusions.

   a. Foreign ownership
   b. Sensitivity analysis
   c. No-bid contract
   d. Policies and procedures

76.

_____ is a systematic method to improve the 'value' of goods or products and services by using an examination of function. Value, as defined, is the ratio of function to cost. Value can therefore be increased by either improving the function or reducing the cost.

a. Cellular manufacturing
b. Capacity planning
c. Master production schedule
d. Value engineering

77. In finance, an _____ is a contract between a buyer and a seller that gives the buyer the right--but not the obligation--to buy or to sell a particular asset (the underlying asset) at a later day at an agreed price. In return for granting the _____, the seller collects a payment (the premium) from the buyer. A call _____ gives the buyer the right to buy the underlying asset; a put _____ gives the buyer of the _____ the right to sell the underlying asset.
   a. A4e
   b. A Stake in the Outcome
   c. AAAI
   d. Option

78. The _____ percentage shows how profitable a company's assets are in generating revenue.

_____ can be computed as:

$$ROA = \frac{\text{Net Income} + \text{Interest Expense} - \text{Interest Tax savings}}{\text{Average Total Assets}}$$

This number tells you what the company can do with what it has, i.e. how many dollars of earnings they derive from each dollar of assets they control. Its a useful number for comparing competing companies in the same industry.

   a. P/E ratio
   b. Return on assets
   c. Return on equity
   d. Return on Capital Employed

79. In business, operating margin, operating income margin, operating profit margin or _____ is the ratio of operating income (operating profit in the UK) divided by net sales, usually presented in percent.

(Relevant figures in italics)

It is a measurement of what proportion of a company's revenue is left over, before taxes and other indirect costs (such as rent, bonus, interest, etc.), after paying for variable costs of production as wages, raw materials, etc. A good operating margin is needed for a company to be able to pay for its fixed costs, such as interest on debt.

   a. Rate of return
   b. Return on equity
   c. P/E ratio
   d. Return on sales

80. In business and accounting, _____s are everything of value that is owned by a person or company. Any property or object of value that one possesses, usually considered as applicable to the payment of one's debts is considered an _____. Simplistically stated, _____s are things of value that can be readily converted into cash.

Chapter 2. CORPORATE-GOVERNANCE BEST PRACTICES

a. A4e
b. AAAI
c. A Stake in the Outcome
d. Asset

81. The _____ is a systematic, interactive forecasting method which relies on a panel of independent experts. The carefully selected experts answer questionnaires in two or more rounds. After each round, a facilitator provides an anonymous summary of the experts' forecasts from the previous round as well as the reasons they provided for their judgments.
   a. Hoshin Kanri
   b. Delphi method
   c. Learning organization
   d. Quality function deployment

82. The National Association of Securities Dealers Automated Quotations known as _____, is an American stock exchange. It is the largest electronic screen-based equity securities trading market in the United States. With approximately 3,800 companies and corporations, it has more trading volume per hour than any other stock exchange in the world.
   a. NASDAQ
   b. 33 Strategies of War
   c. 1990 Clean Air Act
   d. 28-hour day

83. The _____ of 1914, (October 151914, ch. 323, 38 Stat. 730, codified at 15 U.S.C. § 12-27, 29 U.S.C. § 52-53), was enacted in the United States to add further substance to the U.S. antitrust law regime by seeking to prevent anticompetitive practices in their incipiency. That regime started with the Sherman Antitrust Act of 1890, the first Federal law outlawing practices considered harmful to consumers (monopolies and cartels). The Clayton act specified particular prohibited conduct, the three-level enforcement scheme,the exemptions, and the remedial measures.
   a. Long Service Leave
   b. Legal working age
   c. Munn v. Illinois
   d. Clayton Antitrust Act

84. The _____ of 1977 (15 U.S.C. §§ 78dd-1, et seq.) is a United States federal law known primarily for two of its main provisions, one that addresses accounting transparency requirements under the Securities Exchange Act of 1934 and another concerning bribery of foreign officials.
   a. Foreign Corrupt Practices Act
   b. Meritor Savings Bank v. Vinson
   c. Limited liability
   d. Social Security Act of 1965

85. The _____ of 1936 (or Anti-Price Discrimination Act, 15 U.S.C. § 13) is a United States federal law that prohibits what were considered, at the time of passage, to be anticompetitive practices by producers, specifically price discrimination. It grew out of practices in which chain stores were allowed to purchase goods at lower prices than other retailers.
   a. Labor Management Reporting and Disclosure Act
   b. Privity
   c. Robinson-Patman Act
   d. Bona fide occupational qualification

86. The _____ requires the Federal government to investigate and pursue trusts, companies and organizations suspected of violating the Act. It was the first United States Federal statute to limit cartels and monopolies, and today still forms the basis for most antitrust litigation by the federal government.
   a. Sherman Antitrust Act
   b. 33 Strategies of War
   c. 1990 Clean Air Act
   d. 28-hour day

87. An _____ is a practitioner of accountancy, which is the measurement, disclosure or provision of assurance about financial information that helps managers, investors, tax authorities and other decision makers make resource allocation decisions.

Chapter 2. CORPORATE-GOVERNANCE BEST PRACTICES

The word '_____' is derived from the French 'Compter' which took its origin from the Latin 'Computare'. The word was formerly written in English as 'Accomptant', but in process of time the word, which was always pronounced by dropping the 'p', became gradually changed both in pronunciation and in orthography to its present form.

a. A Stake in the Outcome
b. A4e
c. AAAI
d. Accountant

88. The _____ is an independent agency of the United States government, established in 1914 by the _____ Act. Its principal mission is the promotion of 'consumer protection' and the elimination and prevention of what regulators perceive to be harmfully 'anti-competitive' business practices, such as coercive monopoly.

The _____ Act was one of President Wilson's major acts against trusts.

a. 33 Strategies of War
b. 28-hour day
c. 1990 Clean Air Act
d. Federal Trade Commission

89. The _____ of 1914 (15 U.S.C §§ 41-58, as amended) established the Federal Trade Commission (FTC), a bipartisan body of five members appointed by the President of the United States for seven year terms. This Commission was authorized to issue Cease and Desist orders to large corporations to curb unfair trade practices. This Act also gave more flexibility to the US congress for judicial matters.

a. Sarbanes-Oxley Act of 2002
b. Federal Trade Commission Act
c. Resource Conservation and Recovery Act
d. Comprehensive Environmental Response, Compensation, and Liability Act

Chapter 3. CORPORATE-ETHICS BEST PRACTICES

1. In probability theory, a probability distribution is called _____ if its cumulative distribution function is _____. This is equivalent to saying that for random variables X with the distribution in question, Pr[X = a] = 0 for all real numbers a, i.e.: the probability that X attains the value a is zero, for any number a. If the distribution of X is _____ then X is called a _____ random variable.

 a. Continuous
 b. Connectionist expert systems
 c. Decision tree pruning
 d. Pay Band

2. _____ is a management process whereby delivery (customer valued) processes are constantly evaluated and improved in the light of their efficiency, effectiveness and flexibility.

Some see it as a meta process for most management systems (Business Process Management, Quality Management, Project Management). Deming saw it as part of the 'system' whereby feedback from the process and customer were evaluated against organisational goals.

 a. Critical Success Factor
 b. First-mover advantage
 c. Sole proprietorship
 d. Continuous Improvement Process

3. _____ is the principle that the government must respect all of the legal rights that are owed to a person according to the law of the land. As developed through a large body of case law in the United States, this principle gives individuals a varying ability to enforce their rights against alleged violations by governments and their agents (that is, state actors), but normally not against other private citizens.

_____ has also been frequently interpreted as placing limitations on laws and legal proceedings, in order for judges instead of legislators to define and guarantee fundamental fairness, justice, and liberty.

 a. Maximum medical improvement
 b. Due process
 c. Sick leave
 d. Clayton Antitrust Act

4. _____ is a term used for a number of concepts involving either the performance of an investigation of a business or person, or the performance of an act with a certain standard of care. It can be a legal obligation, but the term will more commonly apply to voluntary investigations. A common example of _____ in various industries is the process through which a potential acquirer evaluates a target company or its assets for acquisition.

 a. Negligence in employment
 b. Flextime
 c. Due diligence
 d. Technology transfer

5. The _____ of 2002 (Pub.L. 107-204, 116 Stat. 745, enacted July 30, 2002), also known as the Public Company Accounting Reform and Investor Protection Act of 2002 and commonly called Sarbanes-Oxley, Sarbox or SOX, is a United States federal law enacted on July 30, 2002, as a reaction to a number of major corporate and accounting scandals including those affecting Enron, Tyco International, Adelphia, Peregrine Systems and WorldCom.

 a. Sarbanes-Oxley Act
 b. Fair Labor Standards Act
 c. Letter of credit
 d. Sarbanes-Oxley Act of 2002

6. A _____ occurs when an individual or organization (such as a policeman, lawyer, insurance adjuster, politician, engineer, executive, director of a corporation, medical research scientist, physician, writer, editor, or any other entrusted individual or organization) has an interest that might compromise their actions. The presence of a _____ is independent from the execution of impropriety.

Chapter 3. CORPORATE-ETHICS BEST PRACTICES

In the legal profession, the duty of loyalty owed to a client prohibits an attorney (or a law firm) from representing any other party with interests adverse to those of a current client.

- a. 28-hour day
- b. Global Corruption Report
- c. 1990 Clean Air Act
- d. Conflict of interest

7. _____ is an idea in the field of Organizational studies and management which describes the psychology, attitudes, experiences, beliefs and Values (personal and cultural values) of an organization. It has been defined as 'the specific collection of values and norms that are shared by people and groups in an organization and that control the way they interact with each other and with stakeholders outside the organization.'

This definition continues to explain organizational values also known as 'beliefs and ideas about what kinds of goals members of an organization should pursue and ideas about the appropriate kinds or standards of behavior organizational members should use to achieve these goals. From organizational values develop organizational norms, guidelines or expectations that prescribe appropriate kinds of behavior by employees in particular situations and control the behavior of organizational members towards one another.'

_____ is not the same as corporate culture.

- a. Union shop
- b. Organizational culture
- c. Organizational effectiveness
- d. Organizational development

8. The _____ is a politically conservative group of chief executive officers of major U.S. corporations formed to promote pro-business public policy.

The group was formed in 1972 through the merger of three existing organizations: the March Group, consisting of chief executive officers who met informally to consider public policy issues; the Construction Users Anti-Inflation Roundtable, a group devoted to containing construction costs; and the Labor Law Study Committee, largely made up of labor relations executives of major companies.

It 'strongly supported passage of the' No Child Left Behind Act of 2002, 'and is now actively working with states on implementation.' It has issued press releases, submitted editorials, given congressional testimony and distributed position ads.

- a. Process-based management
- b. Headquarters
- c. National Association for the Advancement of Colored People
- d. Business Roundtable

9. _____ is an advertisement in which a particular product specifically mentions a competitor by name for the express purpose of showing why the competitor is inferior to the product naming it.

Chapter 3. CORPORATE-ETHICS BEST PRACTICES

This should not be confused with parody advertisements, where a fictional product is being advertised for the purpose of poking fun at the particular advertisement, nor should it be confused with the use of a coined brand name for the purpose of comparing the product without actually naming an actual competitor. ('Wikipedia tastes better and is less filling than the Encyclopedia Galactica.')

In the 1980s, during what has been referred to as the cola wars, soft-drink manufacturer Pepsi ran a series of advertisements where people, caught on hidden camera, in a blind taste test, chose Pepsi over rival Coca-Cola.

- a. 33 Strategies of War
- b. Comparative advertising
- c. 1990 Clean Air Act
- d. 28-hour day

10. A mutual _____ or stockholder is an individual or company (including a corporation) that legally owns one or more shares of stock in a joint stock company. A company's _____s collectively own that company. Thus, the typical goal of such companies is to enhance _____ value.
- a. Free riding
- b. Stockholder
- c. Shareholder
- d. 1990 Clean Air Act

11. An _____ is any party that makes an investment.

The term has taken on a specific meaning in finance to describe the particular types of people and companies that regularly purchase equity or debt securities for financial gain in exchange for funding an expanding company. Less frequently, the term is applied to parties who purchase real estate, currency, commodity derivatives, personal property, or other assets.

- a. AAAI
- b. A4e
- c. A Stake in the Outcome
- d. Investor

12. _____ are formal records of the financial activities of a business, person, or other entity. In British English, including United Kingdom company law, _____ are often referred to as accounts, although the term _____ is also used, particularly by accountants.

_____ provide an overview of a business or person's financial condition in both short and long term.

- a. 1990 Clean Air Act
- b. 28-hour day
- c. 33 Strategies of War
- d. Financial statements

13. The National Association of Securities Dealers Automated Quotations known as _____, is an American stock exchange. It is the largest electronic screen-based equity securities trading market in the United States. With approximately 3,800 companies and corporations, it has more trading volume per hour than any other stock exchange in the world.
- a. 28-hour day
- b. 33 Strategies of War
- c. NASDAQ
- d. 1990 Clean Air Act

Chapter 3. CORPORATE-ETHICS BEST PRACTICES

14. _____ is the set of processes, customs, policies, laws, and institutions affecting the way a corporation (or company) is directed, administered or controlled. _____ also includes the relationships among the many stakeholders involved and the goals for which the corporation is governed. The principal stakeholders are the shareholders/members, management, and the board of directors.
   a. Flextime
   b. Guarantee
   c. No-FEAR Act
   d. Corporate governance

15. _____ is an increasingly broadening term with which an organization, or other human system describes the combination of traditionally administrative personnel functions with acquisition and application of skills, knowledge and experience, Employee Relations and resource planning at various levels. The field draws upon concepts developed in Industrial/Organizational Psychology and System Theory. _____ has at least two related interpretations depending on context. The original usage derives from political economy and economics, where it was traditionally called labor, one of four factors of production although this perspective is changing as a function of new and ongoing research into more strategic approaches at national levels. This first usage is used more in terms of '_____ development', and can go beyond just organizations to the level of nations . The more traditional usage within corporations and businesses refers to the individuals within a firm or agency, and to the portion of the organization that deals with hiring, firing, training, and other personnel issues, typically referred to as `_____ management'.
   a. Progressive discipline
   b. Human resource management
   c. Human resources
   d. Bradford Factor

16. A _____ or labor union is an organization of workers who have banded together to achieve common goals in key areas and working conditions. The _____, through its leadership, bargains with the employer on behalf of union members (rank and file members) and negotiates labor contracts (Collective bargaining) with employers. This may include the negotiation of wages, work rules, complaint procedures, rules governing hiring, firing and promotion of workers, benefits, workplace safety and policies.
   a. Company union
   b. Labour law
   c. Working time
   d. Trade union

17. A _____ is a person who alleges misconduct. More complex definitions may be used, but the issue is that the _____ usually faces reprisal. The misconduct may be classified in many ways; for example, a violation of a law, rule, regulation and/or a direct threat to public interest, such as fraud, health/safety violations, and corruption.
   a. 28-hour day
   b. 33 Strategies of War
   c. 1990 Clean Air Act
   d. Whistleblower

18. A _____ is the belief that there is a technique, method, process, activity, incentive or reward that is more effective at delivering a particular outcome than any other technique, method, process, etc. The idea is that with proper processes, checks, and testing, a desired outcome can be delivered with fewer problems and unforeseen complications. _____s can also be defined as the most efficient (least amount of effort) and effective (best results) way of accomplishing a task, based on repeatable procedures that have proven themselves over time for large numbers of people.
   a. Design management
   b. Fix it twice
   c. Best practice
   d. Hierarchical organization

19. _____ is a structured approach to transitioning individuals, teams, and organizations from a current state to a desired future state. The current definition of _____ includes both organizational _____ processes and individual _____ models, which together are used to manage the people side of change.

Chapter 3. CORPORATE-ETHICS BEST PRACTICES

A number of models are available for understanding the transitioning of individuals through the phases of _____ and strengthening organizational development initiative in both government and corporate sectors.

a. 33 Strategies of War
b. 28-hour day
c. 1990 Clean Air Act
d. Change management

20. _____ describes the goal that corporations or public agencies aspire to in their efforts to ensure that personnel are aware of and take steps to comply with relevant laws and regulations.

The International Organisation for Standardisation (ISO) produces international standards such as ISO17799. The International Electrotechnical Commission (IEC) produces international standards in the electrotechnology area.

a. Regulatory compliance
b. Copyright Act of 1976
c. Civil Rights Act of 1991
d. Social Security Act of 1965

21. The _____ is a 1935 United States federal law that limits the means with which employers may react to workers in the private sector that organize labor unions, engage in collective bargaining, and take part in strikes and other forms of concerted activity in support of their demands. The Act does not, on the other hand, cover those workers who are covered by the Railway Labor Act, agricultural employees, domestic employees, supervisors, independent contractors and some close relatives of individual employers.

It was in a context of severe economic troubles that the Wagner Act came into effect.

a. 1990 Clean Air Act
b. 33 Strategies of War
c. National Labor Relations Act
d. 28-hour day

22. The U.S. _____ is an independent agency of the United States government which holds primary responsibility for enforcing the federal securities laws and regulating the securities industry, the nation's stock and options exchanges, and other electronic securities markets. The SEC was created by section 4 of the Securities Exchange Act of 1934 (now codified as 15 U.S.C. Â§ 78d and commonly referred to as the 1934 Act.)

a. 33 Strategies of War
b. Securities and Exchange Commission
c. 28-hour day
d. 1990 Clean Air Act

23. A _____ is a set of instructions having the force of a directive, covering those features of operations that lend themselves to a definite or standardized procedure without loss of effectiveness. Standard Operating Policies and Procedures can be effective catalysts to drive performance improvement and improving organizational results.

a. 1990 Clean Air Act
b. Standard operating procedure
c. Risk-benefit analysis
d. Longitudinal study

24. A Purchasing Manager is an employee within a company, business or other organization who is responsible at some level for buying or approving the acquisition of goods and services needed by the company. The position responsibilities may be the same as that of a buyer or _____, or may include wider supervisory or managerial responsibilities. A Purchasing Manager may oversee the acquisition of materials needed for production, general supplies for offices and facilities, equipment, or construction contracts.

Chapter 3. CORPORATE-ETHICS BEST PRACTICES

a. Purchasing agent
c. Purchasing manager
b. CEO
d. Director of communications

25. _____ is an integrated communications-based process through which individuals and communities discover that existing and newly-identified needs and wants may be satisfied by the products and services of others.

_____ is defined by the American _____ Association as the activity, set of institutions, and processes for creating, communicating, delivering, and exchanging offerings that have value for customers, clients, partners, and society at large. The term developed from the original meaning which referred literally to going to market, as in shopping, or going to a market to buy or sell goods or services.

a. Customer relationship management
c. Disruptive technology
b. Market development
d. Marketing

26. The phrase _____ refers to the aspect of corporate strategy, corporate finance and management dealing with the buying, selling and combining of different companies that can aid, finance, or help a growing company in a given industry grow rapidly without having to create another business entity.

An acquisition, also known as a takeover or a buyout, is the buying of one company (the 'target') by another. An acquisition may be friendly or hostile.

a. 1990 Clean Air Act
c. 33 Strategies of War
b. Mergers and acquisitions
d. 28-hour day

27. The phrase mergers and _____s refers to the aspect of corporate strategy, corporate finance and management dealing with the buying, selling and combining of different companies that can aid, finance, or help a growing company in a given industry grow rapidly without having to create another business entity.

An _____, also known as a takeover or a buyout, is the buying of one company (the 'target') by another. An _____ may be friendly or hostile.

a. Acquisition
c. A Stake in the Outcome
b. AAAI
d. A4e

28. The _____ of 1977 (15 U.S.C. §§ 78dd-1, et seq.) is a United States federal law known primarily for two of its main provisions, one that addresses accounting transparency requirements under the Securities Exchange Act of 1934 and another concerning bribery of foreign officials.

a. Foreign Corrupt Practices Act
c. Social Security Act of 1965
b. Limited liability
d. Meritor Savings Bank v. Vinson

29. _____ is a contract between two parties, one being the employer and the other being the employee. An employee may be defined as: 'A person in the service of another under any contract of hire, express or implied, oral or written, where the employer has the power or right to control and direct the employee in the material details of how the work is to be performed.' Black's Law Dictionary page 471 (5th ed. 1979.)

Chapter 3. CORPORATE-ETHICS BEST PRACTICES

a. Employment rate
b. Exit interview
c. Employment counsellor
d. Employment

30. The term _____ was created by President Lyndon B. Johnson when he signed Executive Order 11246 on September 24, 1965, created to prohibit federal contractors from discriminating against employees on the basis of race, sex, creed, religion, color, or national origin. In more recent times, most employers have also added sexual orientation to the list of non-discrimination.

The Executive Order also required contractors to implement affirmative action plans to increase the participation of minorities and women in the workplace.

a. Equal Employment Opportunity
b. A4e
c. AAAI
d. A Stake in the Outcome

31. The U.S. _____ is a federal agency whose goal is ending employment discrimination. The _____ investigates discrimination complaints based on an individual's race, color, national origin, religion, sex, age, disability and retaliation for reporting and/or opposing a discriminatory practice. The Commission is also tasked with filing suits on behalf of alleged victim(s) of discrimination against employers and as an adjudicatory for claims of discrimination brought against federal agencies.

a. Equal Employment Opportunity Commission
b. Airbus SAS
c. Airbus Industrie
d. ARCO

32. The _____ of 1914, (October 151914, ch. 323, 38 Stat. 730, codified at 15 U.S.C. § 12-27, 29 U.S.C. § 52-53), was enacted in the United States to add further substance to the U.S. antitrust law regime by seeking to prevent anticompetitive practices in their incipiency. That regime started with the Sherman Antitrust Act of 1890, the first Federal law outlawing practices considered harmful to consumers (monopolies and cartels). The Clayton act specified particular prohibited conduct, the three-level enforcement scheme, the exemptions, and the remedial measures.

a. Munn v. Illinois
b. Legal working age
c. Long Service Leave
d. Clayton Antitrust Act

33. The _____ is an independent agency of the United States government, established in 1914 by the _____ Act. Its principal mission is the promotion of 'consumer protection' and the elimination and prevention of what regulators perceive to be harmfully 'anti-competitive' business practices, such as coercive monopoly.

The _____ Act was one of President Wilson's major acts against trusts.

a. 28-hour day
b. 1990 Clean Air Act
c. 33 Strategies of War
d. Federal Trade Commission

34. The _____ of 1914 (15 U.S.C §§ 41-58, as amended) established the Federal Trade Commission (FTC), a bipartisan body of five members appointed by the President of the United States for seven year terms. This Commission was authorized to issue Cease and Desist orders to large corporations to curb unfair trade practices. This Act also gave more flexibility to the US congress for judicial matters.

Chapter 3. CORPORATE-ETHICS BEST PRACTICES

a. Sarbanes-Oxley Act of 2002

b. Comprehensive Environmental Response, Compensation, and Liability Act

c. Resource Conservation and Recovery Act

d. Federal Trade Commission Act

35. The _____ of 1936 (or Anti-Price Discrimination Act, 15 U.S.C. § 13) is a United States federal law that prohibits what were considered, at the time of passage, to be anticompetitive practices by producers, specifically price discrimination. It grew out of practices in which chain stores were allowed to purchase goods at lower prices than other retailers.

a. Labor Management Reporting and Disclosure Act
b. Privity
c. Bona fide occupational qualification
d. Robinson-Patman Act

36. The _____ requires the Federal government to investigate and pursue trusts, companies and organizations suspected of violating the Act. It was the first United States Federal statute to limit cartels and monopolies, and today still forms the basis for most antitrust litigation by the federal government.

a. 33 Strategies of War
b. 1990 Clean Air Act
c. 28-hour day
d. Sherman Antitrust Act

37. The general definition of an _____ is an evaluation of a person, organization, system, process, project or product. _____s are performed to ascertain the validity and reliability of information; also to provide an assessment of a system's internal control. The goal of an _____ is to express an opinion on the person / organization/system (etc) in question, under evaluation based on work done on a test basis.

a. A Stake in the Outcome
b. Audit committee
c. Internal control
d. Audit

38. In a publicly-held company, an _____ is an operating committee of the Board of Directors, typically charged with oversight of financial reporting and disclosure. Committee members are drawn from members of the Company's board of directors, with a Chairperson selected from among the members. An _____ of a publicly-traded company in the United States is composed of independent and outside directors referred to as non-executive directors, at least one of which is typically a financial expert.

a. Internal control
b. A Stake in the Outcome
c. Audit committee
d. Internal auditing

39. _____ refers to the movement of cash into or out of a business or financial product. It is usually measured during a specified, finite period of time. Measurement of _____ can be used

- to determine a project's rate of return or value. The time of _____s into and out of projects are used as inputs in financial models such as internal rate of return, and net present value.
- to determine problems with a business's liquidity. Being profitable does not necessarily mean being liquid. A company can fail because of a shortage of cash, even while profitable.
- as an alternate measure of a business's profits when it is believed that accrual accounting concepts do not represent economic realities. For example, a company may be notionally profitable but generating little operational cash (as may be the case for a company that barters its products rather than selling for cash.) In such a case, the company may be deriving additional operating cash by issuing shares evaluating default risk, re-investment requirements, etc.

_____ is a generic term used differently depending on the context. It may be defined by users for their own purposes.

a. Gross profit margin
b. Gross profit
c. Sweat equity
d. Cash flow

40. _____ is the discipline of planning, organizing and managing resources to bring about the successful completion of specific project goals and objectives. It is often closely related to and sometimes conflated with Program management.

A project is a finite endeavor--having specific start and completion dates--undertaken to meet particular goals and objectives, usually to bring about beneficial change or added value.

a. Project engineer
b. Project management
c. Precedence diagram
d. Work package

Chapter 4. GENERAL-MANAGEMENT BEST PRACTICES

1. _____ generally refers to a list of all planned expenses and revenues. It is a plan for saving and spending. A _____ is an important concept in microeconomics, which uses a _____ line to illustrate the trade-offs between two or more goods.

   a. 1990 Clean Air Act
   b. 28-hour day
   c. 33 Strategies of War
   d. Budget

2. _____ for short is a descriptive term for certain executives in a business operation. It is also a formal title held by some business executives, most commonly in the hospitality industry.

   A _____ has broad, overall responsibility for a business or organization. Whereas a manager may be responsible for one functional area, the _____ is responsible for all areas.

   a. Managing director
   b. Chief technology officer
   c. Chief knowledge officer
   d. General manager

3. _____ is a structured approach to transitioning individuals, teams, and organizations from a current state to a desired future state. The current definition of _____ includes both organizational _____ processes and individual _____ models, which together are used to manage the people side of change.

   A number of models are available for understanding the transitioning of individuals through the phases of _____ and strengthening organizational development initiative in both government and corporate sectors.

   a. 33 Strategies of War
   b. 1990 Clean Air Act
   c. 28-hour day
   d. Change management

4. _____ is the process by which an organization deals with any major unpredictable event that threatens to harm the organization, its stakeholders, or the general public. Three elements are common to most definitions of crisis: (a) a threat to the organization, (b) the element of surprise, and (c) a short decision time.

   Whereas risk management involves assessing potential threats and finding the best ways to avoid those threats, _____ involves dealing with the disasters after they have occurred.

   a. Business value
   b. Capability management
   c. C-A-K-E
   d. Crisis management

5. _____ is a process of planning and controlling the performance or execution of any type of activity, such as:

   - a project (project _____) or
   - a process (process _____, sometimes referred to as the process performance measurement and management system.)

   Organization's senior management is responsible for carrying out its _____.

   a. Participatory management
   b. Human Relations Movement
   c. Management process
   d. Work design

Chapter 4. GENERAL-MANAGEMENT BEST PRACTICES

6. A _____ or chief executive is one of the highest-ranking corporate officer (executive) or administrator in charge of total management. An individual selected as President and _____ of a corporation, company, organization, or agency, reports to the board of directors. In internal communication and press releases, many companies capitalize the term and those of other high positions, even when they are not proper nouns.

  a. Chief executive officer
  b. Chief brand officer
  c. Purchasing manager
  d. Financial analyst

7. _____ is an organization's process of defining its strategy and making decisions on allocating its resources to pursue this strategy, including its capital and people. Various business analysis techniques can be used in _____, including SWOT analysis (Strengths, Weaknesses, Opportunities, and Threats) and PEST analysis (Political, Economic, Social, and Technological analysis) or STEER analysis involving Socio-cultural, Technological, Economic, Ecological, and Regulatory factors and EPISTEL (Environment, Political, Informatic, Social, Technological, Economic and Legal)

_____ is the formal consideration of an organization's future course. All _____ deals with at least one of three key questions:

1. 'What do we do?'
2. 'For whom do we do it?'
3. 'How do we excel?'

In business _____, the third question is better phrased 'How can we beat or avoid competition?'. (Bradford and Duncan, page 1.)

  a. Strategic planning
  b. 33 Strategies of War
  c. 1990 Clean Air Act
  d. 28-hour day

8. While _____ literally refers to a person responsible for the performance of duties involved in running an organization, the exact meaning of the role is variable, depending on the organization.

While there is no clear line between executive or principal and inferior officers, principal officers are high-level officials in the executive branch of U.S. government such as department heads of independent agencies. In Humphrey's Executor v. United States, 295 U.S. 602 (1935), the Court distinguished between _____s and quasi-legislative or quasi-judicial officers by stating that the former serve at the pleasure of the President and may be removed at his discretion.

  a. Easement
  b. Executive officer
  c. Australian Fair Pay and Conditions Standard
  d. Unreported employment

9. _____ is a concept in ethics with several meanings. It is often used synonymously with such concepts as responsibility, answerability, enforcement, blameworthiness, liability and other terms associated with the expectation of account-giving. As an aspect of governance, it has been central to discussions related to problems in both the public and private (corporation) worlds.

  a. A Stake in the Outcome
  b. Usury
  c. A4e
  d. Accountability

Chapter 4. GENERAL-MANAGEMENT BEST PRACTICES

10. _____ describes the situation when output from (or information about the result of) an event or phenomenon in the past will influence the same event/phenomenon in the present or future. When an event is part of a chain of cause-and-effect that forms a circuit or loop, then the event is said to 'feed back' into itself.

_____ is also a synonym for:

- _____ signal; the information about the initial event that is the basis for subsequent modification of the event.
- _____ loop; the causal path that leads from the initial generation of the _____ signal to the subsequent modification of the event.

_____ is a mechanism, process or signal that is looped back to control a system within itself. Such a loop is called a _____ loop.

- a. Feedback
- b. Positive feedback
- c. Feedback loop
- d. 1990 Clean Air Act

11. _____ is the acquisition of goods and/or services at the best possible total cost of ownership, in the right quality and quantity, at the right time, in the right place and from the right source for the direct benefit or use of corporations, individuals generally via a contract. Simple _____ may involve nothing more than repeat purchasing. Complex _____ could involve finding long term partners - or even 'co-destiny' suppliers that might fundamentally commit one organization to another.

- a. Procurement
- b. Psychological pricing
- c. Golden parachute
- d. Sole proprietorship

12. _____ is an increasingly broadening term with which an organization, or other human system describes the combination of traditionally administrative personnel functions with acquisition and application of skills, knowledge and experience, Employee Relations and resource planning at various levels. The field draws upon concepts developed in Industrial/Organizational Psychology and System Theory. _____ has at least two related interpretations depending on context. The original usage derives from political economy and economics, where it was traditionally called labor, one of four factors of production although this perspective is changing as a function of new and ongoing research into more strategic approaches at national levels. This first usage is used more in terms of '_____ development', and can go beyond just organizations to the level of nations . The more traditional usage within corporations and businesses refers to the individuals within a firm or agency, and to the portion of the organization that deals with hiring, firing, training, and other personnel issues, typically referred to as `_____ management'.

- a. Progressive discipline
- b. Bradford Factor
- c. Human resource management
- d. Human resources

13. _____ is the concept of how effective an organization is in achieving the outcomes the organization intends to produce. The idea of _____ is especially important for non-profit organizations as most people who donate money to non-profit organizations and charities are interested in knowing whether the organization is effective in accomplishing its goals.

An organization's effectiveness is also dependent on its communicative competence and ethics.

Chapter 4. GENERAL-MANAGEMENT BEST PRACTICES

a. Organizational development
b. Organizational structure
c. Informal organization
d. Organizational effectiveness

14. A _____ is the belief that there is a technique, method, process, activity, incentive or reward that is more effective at delivering a particular outcome than any other technique, method, process, etc. The idea is that with proper processes, checks, and testing, a desired outcome can be delivered with fewer problems and unforeseen complications. _____s can also be defined as the most efficient (least amount of effort) and effective (best results) way of accomplishing a task, based on repeatable procedures that have proven themselves over time for large numbers of people.
   a. Best practice
   b. Design management
   c. Fix it twice
   d. Hierarchical organization

15. _____ is an idea in the field of Organizational studies and management which describes the psychology, attitudes, experiences, beliefs and Values (personal and cultural values) of an organization. It has been defined as 'the specific collection of values and norms that are shared by people and groups in an organization and that control the way they interact with each other and with stakeholders outside the organization.'

This definition continues to explain organizational values also known as 'beliefs and ideas about what kinds of goals members of an organization should pursue and ideas about the appropriate kinds or standards of behavior organizational members should use to achieve these goals. From organizational values develop organizational norms, guidelines or expectations that prescribe appropriate kinds of behavior by employees in particular situations and control the behavior of organizational members towards one another.'

_____ is not the same as corporate culture.

   a. Organizational development
   b. Union shop
   c. Organizational effectiveness
   d. Organizational culture

16. The _____ captures an expanded spectrum of values and criteria for measuring organizational success: economic, ecological and social. With the ratification of the United Nations and ICLEI _____ standard for urban and community accounting in early 2007, this became the dominant approach to public sector full cost accounting. Similar UN standards apply to natural capital and human capital measurement to assist in measurements required by _____, e.g. the ecoBudget standard for reporting ecological footprint.
   a. 28-hour day
   b. 1990 Clean Air Act
   c. 33 Strategies of War
   d. Triple bottom line

17. _____ is one of the managerial functions like planning, organizing, staffing and directing. It is an important function because it helps to check the errors and to take the corrective action so that deviation from standards are minimized and stated goals of the organization are achieved in desired manner.According to modern concepts, _____ is a foreseeing action whereas earlier concept of _____ was used only when errors were detected. _____ in management means setting standards, measuring actual performance and taking corrective action.
   a. Control
   b. Schedule of reinforcement
   c. Turnover
   d. Decision tree pruning

Chapter 4. GENERAL-MANAGEMENT BEST PRACTICES

18. In accounting and auditing, _____ is defined as a process effected by an organization's structure, work and authority flows, people and management information systems, designed to help the organization accomplish specific goals or objectives. It is a means by which an organization's resources are directed, monitored, and measured. It plays an important role in preventing and detecting fraud and protecting the organization's resources, both physical (e.g., machinery and property) and intangible (e.g., reputation or intellectual property such as trademarks.)

   a. A Stake in the Outcome   b. Internal control
   c. Internal auditing   d. Audit committee

19. A _____ is a set of instructions having the force of a directive, covering those features of operations that lend themselves to a definite or standardized procedure without loss of effectiveness. Standard Operating Policies and Procedures can be effective catalysts to drive performance improvement and improving organizational results.

   a. 1990 Clean Air Act   b. Standard operating procedure
   c. Longitudinal study   d. Risk-benefit analysis

20. A _____ or business method is a collection of related, structured activities or tasks that produce a specific service or product (serve a particular goal) for a particular customer or customers. It often can be visualized with a flowchart as a sequence of activities.

There are three types of _____ es:

1. Management processes, the processes that govern the operation of a system. Typical management processes include 'Corporate Governance' and 'Strategic Management'.
2. Operational processes, processes that constitute the core business and create the primary value stream. Typical operational processes are Purchasing, Manufacturing, Marketing, and Sales.
3. Supporting processes, which support the core processes. Examples include Accounting, Recruitment, Technical support.

A _____ begins with a customer's need and ends with a customer's need fulfillment. Process oriented organizations break down the barriers of structural departments and try to avoid functional silos.

   a. 28-hour day   b. 33 Strategies of War
   c. Business process   d. 1990 Clean Air Act

21. _____ is, in computer science and management, an approach aiming at improvements by means of elevating efficiency and effectiveness of the business process that exist within and across organizations. The key to _____ is for organizations to look at their business processes from a 'clean slate' perspective and determine how they can best construct these processes to improve how they conduct business. _____ Cycle.

_____ is also known as _____, Business Process Redesign, Business Transformation, or Business Process Change Management.

   a. Horizontal integration   b. Personal management interview
   c. Business process reengineering   d. Product life cycle

Chapter 4. GENERAL-MANAGEMENT BEST PRACTICES

22. _____ is a business management strategy aimed at embedding awareness of quality in all organizational processes. _____ has been widely used in manufacturing, education, hospitals, call centers, government, and service industries, as well as NASA space and science programs.

As defined by the International Organization for Standardization (ISO):

'_____ is a management approach for an organization, centered on quality, based on the participation of all its members and aiming at long-term success through customer satisfaction, and benefits to all members of the organization and to society.' ISO 8402:1994

One major aim is to reduce variation from every process so that greater consistency of effort is obtained. (Royse, D., Thyer, B., Padgett D., ' Logan T., 2006)

   a. Quality management
   b. 1990 Clean Air Act
   c. Total quality management
   d. 28-hour day

23. _____ can be considered to have three main components: quality control, quality assurance and quality improvement. _____ is focused not only on product quality, but also the means to achieve it. _____ therefore uses quality assurance and control of processes as well as products to achieve more consistent quality.
   a. Total quality management
   b. 1990 Clean Air Act
   c. 28-hour day
   d. Quality management

24. _____ is an inventory strategy that strives to improve the return on investment of a business by reducing in-process inventory and its associated carrying costs. To meet _____ objectives, the process relies on signals between different points in the process. This means the process is often driven by a series of signals, or Kanban, which tell production when to make the next part. Kanban are usually 'tickets' but can be simple visual signals, such as the presence or absence of a part on a shelf. Implemented correctly, _____ can dramatically improve a manufacturing organization's return on investment, quality, and efficiency.
   a. Just-in-time
   b. 33 Strategies of War
   c. 28-hour day
   d. 1990 Clean Air Act

25. _____ or lean production, which is often known simply as 'Lean', is a production practice that considers the expenditure of resources for any goal other than the creation of value for the end customer to be wasteful, and thus a target for elimination. Working from the perspective of the customer who consumes a product or service, 'value' is defined as any action or process that a customer would be willing to pay for. Basically, lean is centered around creating more value with less work.
   a. Production line
   b. Six Sigma
   c. Theory of constraints
   d. Lean manufacturing

26. The general definition of an _____ is an evaluation of a person, organization, system, process, project or product. _____s are performed to ascertain the validity and reliability of information; also to provide an assessment of a system's internal control. The goal of an _____ is to express an opinion on the person / organization/system (etc) in question, under evaluation based on work done on a test basis.
   a. Internal control
   b. Audit
   c. A Stake in the Outcome
   d. Audit committee

Chapter 4. GENERAL-MANAGEMENT BEST PRACTICES

27. _____ or contract administration is the management of contracts made with customers, vendors, partners, or employees. _____ includes negotiating the terms and conditions in contracts and ensuring compliance with the terms and conditions, as well as documenting and agreeing any changes that may arise during its implementation or execution. It can be summarized as the process of systematically and efficiently managing contract creating, execution, and analysis for the purpose of maximizing financial and operational performance and minimizing risk.
   a. World Trade Organization
   b. Network planning and design
   c. 1990 Clean Air Act
   d. Contract management

28. A _____ is a volunteer group composed of workers (or even students), usually under the leadership of their supervisor (but they can elect a team leader), who are trained to identify, analyse and solve work-related problems and present their solutions to management in order to improve the performance of the organization, and motivate and enrich the work of employees. When matured, true _____s become self-managing, having gained the confidence of management. _____s are an alternative to the dehumanising concept of the Division of Labour, where workers or individuals are treated like robots.
   a. Connectionist expert systems
   b. Certified in Production and Inventory Management
   c. Quality circle
   d. Competency-based job descriptions

29. In decision theory and estimation theory, the _____ of an estimator, $\hat{\theta}$, of an unknown parameter of the distribution, θ, is the expected value of the loss function

$$R(\theta, \hat{\theta}) = \mathbb{E}_\theta L(\theta, \hat{\theta}) = \int L(\theta, \hat{\theta}) \, dP_\theta.$$

where dP_θ is a probability measure parametrized by θ.

- For a scalar parameter θ and a quadratic loss function,

$$L(\theta, \hat{\theta}) = (\theta - \hat{\theta})^2$$

the _____ function becomes the mean squared error of the estimate,

$$R(\theta, \hat{\theta}) = E_\theta(\theta - \hat{\theta})^2$$

- In density estimation, the unknown parameter is probability density itself. The loss function is typically chosen to be a norm in an appropriate function space. For example, for L^2 norm,

$$L(f, \hat{f}) = \|f - \hat{f}\|_2^2$$

the _____ function becomes the mean integrated squared error

$$R(f, \hat{f}) = E\|f - \hat{f}\|^2$$

a. Linear model
b. Risk
c. Financial modeling
d. Risk aversion

30. _____ is the identification, assessment, and prioritization of risks followed by coordinated and economical application of resources to minimize, monitor, and control the probability and/or impact of unfortunate events.. Risks can come from uncertainty in financial markets, project failures, legal liabilities, credit risk, accidents, natural causes and disasters as well as deliberate attacks from an adversary. Several _____ standards have been developed including the Project Management Institute, the National Institute of Science and Technology, actuarial societies, and ISO standards.

a. Kanban
b. Trademark
c. Succession planning
d. Risk management

31. _____ is an advertisement in which a particular product specifically mentions a competitor by name for the express purpose of showing why the competitor is inferior to the product naming it.

This should not be confused with parody advertisements, where a fictional product is being advertised for the purpose of poking fun at the particular advertisement, nor should it be confused with the use of a coined brand name for the purpose of comparing the product without actually naming an actual competitor. ('Wikipedia tastes better and is less filling than the Encyclopedia Galactica.')

In the 1980s, during what has been referred to as the cola wars, soft-drink manufacturer Pepsi ran a series of advertisements where people, caught on hidden camera, in a blind taste test, chose Pepsi over rival Coca-Cola.

Chapter 4. GENERAL-MANAGEMENT BEST PRACTICES

a. 33 Strategies of War
b. Comparative advertising
c. 28-hour day
d. 1990 Clean Air Act

32. The phrase mergers and _____s refers to the aspect of corporate strategy, corporate finance and management dealing with the buying, selling and combining of different companies that can aid, finance, or help a growing company in a given industry grow rapidly without having to create another business entity.

An _____, also known as a takeover or a buyout, is the buying of one company (the 'target') by another. An _____ may be friendly or hostile.

a. A4e
b. AAAI
c. A Stake in the Outcome
d. Acquisition

33. The _____ of 1914, (October 151914, ch. 323, 38 Stat. 730, codified at 15 U.S.C. §§ 12-27, 29 U.S.C. §§ 52-53), was enacted in the United States to add further substance to the U.S. antitrust law regime by seeking to prevent anticompetitive practices in their incipiency. That regime started with the Sherman Antitrust Act of 1890, the first Federal law outlawing practices considered harmful to consumers (monopolies and cartels). The Clayton act specified particular prohibited conduct, the three-level enforcement scheme,the exemptions, and the remedial measures.

a. Clayton Antitrust Act
b. Long Service Leave
c. Munn v. Illinois
d. Legal working age

34. The _____ is an independent agency of the United States government, established in 1914 by the _____ Act. Its principal mission is the promotion of 'consumer protection' and the elimination and prevention of what regulators perceive to be harmfully 'anti-competitive' business practices, such as coercive monopoly.

The _____ Act was one of President Wilson's major acts against trusts.

a. 1990 Clean Air Act
b. 28-hour day
c. 33 Strategies of War
d. Federal Trade Commission

35. The _____ of 1914 (15 U.S.C §§ 41-58, as amended) established the Federal Trade Commission (FTC), a bipartisan body of five members appointed by the President of the United States for seven year terms. This Commission was authorized to issue Cease and Desist orders to large corporations to curb unfair trade practices. This Act also gave more flexibility to the US congress for judicial matters.

a. Resource Conservation and Recovery Act
b. Comprehensive Environmental Response, Compensation, and Liability Act
c. Sarbanes-Oxley Act of 2002
d. Federal Trade Commission Act

36. The _____ of 1936 (or Anti-Price Discrimination Act, 15 U.S.C. § 13) is a United States federal law that prohibits what were considered, at the time of passage, to be anticompetitive practices by producers, specifically price discrimination. It grew out of practices in which chain stores were allowed to purchase goods at lower prices than other retailers.

a. Bona fide occupational qualification
b. Robinson-Patman Act
c. Labor Management Reporting and Disclosure Act
d. Privity

Chapter 4. GENERAL-MANAGEMENT BEST PRACTICES

37. The _____ requires the Federal government to investigate and pursue trusts, companies and organizations suspected of violating the Act. It was the first United States Federal statute to limit cartels and monopolies, and today still forms the basis for most antitrust litigation by the federal government.
   a. 1990 Clean Air Act
   b. 28-hour day
   c. 33 Strategies of War
   d. Sherman Antitrust Act

38. The _____, first published in 1952, is one of a number of uniform acts that have been promulgated in conjunction with efforts to harmonize the law of sales and other commercial transactions in all 50 states within the United States of America. This objective is deemed important because of the prevalence of commercial transactions that extend beyond one state (for example, where the goods are manufactured in state A, warehoused in state B, sold from state C and delivered in state D.) The _____ deals primarily with transactions involving personal property (movable property), not real property (immovable property.)
   a. AAAI
   b. A4e
   c. A Stake in the Outcome
   d. Uniform Commercial Code

Chapter 5. MANUFACTURING- AND SERVICE-MANAGEMENT BEST PRACTICES

1. A _____ or chief operations officer is a corporate officer responsible for managing the day-to-day activities of the corporation and for operations management (OM.) The _____ is one of the highest-ranking members of an organization's senior management, monitoring the daily operations of the company and reporting to the board of directors and the top executive officer, usually the chief executive officer (CEO.) The _____ is usually an executive or senior officer.
   a. Value based pricing
   b. Supervisory board
   c. Product innovation
   d. Chief operating officer

2. The _____ or gross domestic income (GDI), a basic measure of an economy's economic performance, is the market value of all final goods and services made within the borders of a nation in a year. _____ can be defined in three ways, all of which are conceptually identical. First, it is equal to the total expenditures for all final goods and services produced within the country in a stipulated period of time (usually a 365-day year).
   a. Gross domestic product
   b. Human capital
   c. Perfect competition
   d. Productivity management

3. _____ is an advertisement in which a particular product specifically mentions a competitor by name for the express purpose of showing why the competitor is inferior to the product naming it.

This should not be confused with parody advertisements, where a fictional product is being advertised for the purpose of poking fun at the particular advertisement, nor should it be confused with the use of a coined brand name for the purpose of comparing the product without actually naming an actual competitor. ('Wikipedia tastes better and is less filling than the Encyclopedia Galactica.')

In the 1980s, during what has been referred to as the cola wars, soft-drink manufacturer Pepsi ran a series of advertisements where people, caught on hidden camera, in a blind taste test, chose Pepsi over rival Coca-Cola.

   a. 33 Strategies of War
   b. 1990 Clean Air Act
   c. Comparative advertising
   d. 28-hour day

4. _____ is the process of comparing the cost, cycle time, productivity, or quality of a specific process or method to another that is widely considered to be an industry standard or best practice. Essentially, _____ provides a snapshot of the performance of your business and helps you understand where you are in relation to a particular standard. The result is often a business case for making changes in order to make improvements.
   a. Complementors
   b. Cost leadership
   c. Competitive heterogeneity
   d. Benchmarking

5. _____ is the design of all information-gathering exercises where variation is present, whether under the full control of the experimenter or not. (The latter situation is usually called an observational study.) Often the experimenter is interested in the effect of some process or intervention (the 'treatment') on some objects (the 'experimental units'), which may be people, parts of people, groups of people, etc.
   a. Design of experiments
   b. 28-hour day
   c. Taguchi methods
   d. 1990 Clean Air Act

6. The _____, widely known as ISO , is an international-standard-setting body composed of representatives from various national standards organizations. Founded on 23 February 1947, the organization promulgates worldwide proprietary industrial and commercial standards. It is headquartered in Geneva, Switzerland.

Chapter 5. MANUFACTURING- AND SERVICE-MANAGEMENT BEST PRACTICES

a. International Organization for Standardization
b. A4e
c. AAAI
d. A Stake in the Outcome

7. _____ is an inventory strategy that strives to improve the return on investment of a business by reducing in-process inventory and its associated carrying costs. To meet _____ objectives, the process relies on signals between different points in the process. This means the process is often driven by a series of signals, or Kanban , which tell production when to make the next part. Kanban are usually 'tickets' but can be simple visual signals, such as the presence or absence of a part on a shelf. Implemented correctly, _____ can dramatically improve a manufacturing organization's return on investment, quality, and efficiency.

a. 1990 Clean Air Act
b. 28-hour day
c. 33 Strategies of War
d. Just-in-time

8. _____ or lean production, which is often known simply as 'Lean', is a production practice that considers the expenditure of resources for any goal other than the creation of value for the end customer to be wasteful, and thus a target for elimination. Working from the perspective of the customer who consumes a product or service, 'value' is defined as any action or process that a customer would be willing to pay for. Basically, lean is centered around creating more value with less work.

a. Theory of constraints
b. Six Sigma
c. Production line
d. Lean manufacturing

9. _____ is a 'method to transform user demands into design quality, to deploy the functions forming quality, and to deploy methods for achieving the design quality into subsystems and component parts, and ultimately to specific elements of the manufacturing process.' , as described by Dr. Yoji Akao, who originally developed _____ in Japan in 1966, when the author combined his work in quality assurance and quality control points with function deployment used in Value Engineering.

_____ is designed to help planners focus on characteristics of a new or existing product or service from the viewpoints of market segments, company, or technology-development needs. The technique yields graphs and matrices.

a. Learning organization
b. 1990 Clean Air Act
c. Hoshin Kanri
d. Quality function deployment

10. _____ is a business management strategy, initially implemented by Motorola, that today enjoys widespread application in many sectors of industry.

_____ seeks to improve the quality of process outputs by identifying and removing the causes of defects (errors) and variation in manufacturing and business processes. It uses a set of quality management methods, including statistical methods, and creates a special infrastructure of people within the organization ('Black Belts' etc.)

a. Takt time
b. Theory of constraints
c. Production line
d. Six Sigma

Chapter 5. MANUFACTURING- AND SERVICE-MANAGEMENT BEST PRACTICES

11. _____ is an effective method of monitoring a process through the use of control charts. Control charts enable the use of objective criteria for distinguishing background variation from events of significance based on statistical techniques. Much of its power lies in the ability to monitor both process center and its variation about that center.
   a. Process capability
   b. Single Minute Exchange of Die
   c. Quality control
   d. Statistical process control

12. _____ are statistical methods developed by Genichi Taguchi to improve the quality of manufactured goods, and more recently also applied to biotechnology, marketing and advertising. Professional statisticians have welcomed the goals and improvements brought about by _____, particularly by Taguchi's development of designs for studying variation, but have criticized the inefficiency of some of Taguchi's proposals.

Taguchi's work includes three principal contributions to statistics:

1. Taguchi loss function;
2. The philosophy of off-line quality control; and
3. Innovations in the design of experiments.

Traditionally, statistical methods have relied on mean-unbiased estimators of treatment effects: Under the conditions of the Gauss-Markov theorem, least squares estimators have minimum variance among all mean-unbiased estimators. The emphasis on comparisons of means also draws (limiting) comfort from the law of large numbers, according to which the sample means converge to the true mean.

   a. 28-hour day
   b. Taguchi methods
   c. Design of experiments
   d. 1990 Clean Air Act

13. _____ is an overall management philosophy introduced by Dr. Eliyahu M. Goldratt in his 1984 book titled The Goal, that is geared to help organizations continually achieve their goal. The title comes from the contention that any manageable system is limited in achieving more of its goal by a very small number of constraints, and that there is always at least one constraint. The _____ process seeks to identify the constraint and restructure the rest of the organization around it, through the use of the Five Focusing Steps.
   a. Takt time
   b. Six Sigma
   c. Production line
   d. Theory of constraints

14. _____ is a term used in business and Information Technology (through ITIL) to describe the process of capturing a customer's requirements. Specifically, the _____ is a market research technique that produces a detailed set of customer wants and needs, organized into a hierarchical structure, and then prioritized in terms of relative importance and satisfaction with current alternatives. _____ studies typically consist of both qualitative and quantitative research steps.
   a. Board of governors
   b. Business philosophy
   c. Goal setting
   d. Voice of the customer

15. _____ is one of the managerial functions like planning, organizing, staffing and directing. It is an important function because it helps to check the errors and to take the corrective action so that deviation from standards are minimized and stated goals of the organization are achieved in desired manner. According to modern concepts, _____ is a foreseeing action whereas earlier concept of _____ was used only when errors were detected. _____ in management means setting standards, measuring actual performance and taking corrective action.

Chapter 5. MANUFACTURING- AND SERVICE-MANAGEMENT BEST PRACTICES

a. Decision tree pruning
b. Schedule of reinforcement
c. Turnover
d. Control

16. _____ can be considered to have three main components: quality control, quality assurance and quality improvement. _____ is focused not only on product quality, but also the means to achieve it. _____ therefore uses quality assurance and control of processes as well as products to achieve more consistent quality.
    a. 1990 Clean Air Act
    b. 28-hour day
    c. Total quality management
    d. Quality management

17. The general definition of an _____ is an evaluation of a person, organization, system, process, project or product. _____s are performed to ascertain the validity and reliability of information; also to provide an assessment of a system's internal control. The goal of an _____ is to express an opinion on the person / organization/system (etc) in question, under evaluation based on work done on a test basis.
    a. A Stake in the Outcome
    b. Audit committee
    c. Internal control
    d. Audit

18. A _____ is a volunteer group composed of workers (or even students), usually under the leadership of their supervisor (but they can elect a team leader), who are trained to identify, analyse and solve work-related problems and present their solutions to management in order to improve the performance of the organization, and motivate and enrich the work of employees. When matured, true _____s become self-managing, having gained the confidence of management. _____s are an alternative to the dehumanising concept of the Division of Labour, where workers or individuals are treated like robots.
    a. Competency-based job descriptions
    b. Quality circle
    c. Certified in Production and Inventory Management
    d. Connectionist expert systems

19. A _____ or business method is a collection of related, structured activities or tasks that produce a specific service or product (serve a particular goal) for a particular customer or customers. It often can be visualized with a flowchart as a sequence of activities.

There are three types of _____es:

1. Management processes, the processes that govern the operation of a system. Typical management processes include 'Corporate Governance' and 'Strategic Management'.
2. Operational processes, processes that constitute the core business and create the primary value stream. Typical operational processes are Purchasing, Manufacturing, Marketing, and Sales.
3. Supporting processes, which support the core processes. Examples include Accounting, Recruitment, Technical support.

A _____ begins with a customer's need and ends with a customer's need fulfillment. Process oriented organizations break down the barriers of structural departments and try to avoid functional silos.

a. 1990 Clean Air Act
b. 28-hour day
c. 33 Strategies of War
d. Business process

Chapter 5. MANUFACTURING- AND SERVICE-MANAGEMENT BEST PRACTICES

20. _____ is a work methodology based on the parallelization of tasks (ie. concurrently.) It refers to an approach used in product development in which functions of design engineering, manufacturing engineering and other functions are integrated to reduce the elapsed time required to bring a new product to the market.

  a. Critical Chain Project Management   b. Project management

  c. Work package   d. Concurrent engineering

21. _____ is subcontracting a process, such as product design or manufacturing, to a third-party company. The decision to outsource is often made in the interest of lowering cost or making better use of time and energy costs, redirecting or conserving energy directed at the competencies of a particular business, or to make more efficient use of land, labor, capital, (information) technology and resources. _____ became part of the business lexicon during the 1980s.

  a. Operant conditioning   b. Unemployment insurance

  c. Outsourcing   d. Opinion leadership

22. In economics, business, retail, and accounting, a _____ is the value of money that has been used up to produce something, and hence is not available for use anymore. In economics, a _____ is an alternative that is given up as a result of a decision. In business, the _____ may be one of acquisition, in which case the amount of money expended to acquire it is counted as _____.

  a. Cost   b. Cost allocation

  c. Cost overrun   d. Fixed costs

23. The concept of quality costs is a means to quantify the total _____-related efforts and deficiencies. It was first described by Armand V. Feigenbaum in a 1956 Harvard Business Review article.

Prior to its introduction, the general perception was that higher quality requires higher costs, either by buying better materials or machines or by hiring more labor.

  a. Fixed costs   b. Quality costs

  c. Cost of quality   d. Cost accounting

24. _____ is, in very basic words, a position a firm occupies against its competitors.

According to Michael Porter, the three methods for creating a sustainable _____ are through:

1. Cost leadership

2. Differentiation

3. Focus (economics)

  a. Competitive advantage   b. 28-hour day

  c. Theory Z   d. 1990 Clean Air Act

25. _____ is an integrated communications-based process through which individuals and communities discover that existing and newly-identified needs and wants may be satisfied by the products and services of others.

_____ is defined by the American _____ Association as the activity, set of institutions, and processes for creating, communicating, delivering, and exchanging offerings that have value for customers, clients, partners, and society at large. The term developed from the original meaning which referred literally to going to market, as in shopping, or going to a market to buy or sell goods or services.

a. Market development
b. Disruptive technology
c. Marketing
d. Customer relationship management

26. _____ is the term used to refer to the standard framework of guidelines for financial accounting used in any given jurisdiction. _____ includes the standards, conventions, and rules accountants follow in recording and summarizing transactions, and in the preparation of financial statements.

Financial accounting is information that must be assembled and reported objectively.

a. Generally accepted accounting principles
b. Depreciation
c. Treasury stock
d. Net income

27. _____ is the management of the flow of goods, information and other resources, including energy and people, between the point of origin and the point of consumption in order to meet the requirements of consumers (frequently, and originally, military organizations.) _____ involves the integration of information, transportation, inventory, warehousing, material-handling, and packaging, and occasionally security. _____ is a channel of the supply chain which adds the value of time and place utility.

a. Logistics
b. 28-hour day
c. Third-party logistics
d. 1990 Clean Air Act

28. The term _____ is that part of Supply Chain Management that plans, implements, and controls the efficient, effective, forward, and reverse flow and storage of goods, services, and related information between the point of origin and the point of consumption in order to meet customers' requirements.

Software is used for logistics automation which helps the supply chain industry in automating the work flow as well as management of the system. There are very few generalized software available in the new market in the said topology.

a. Dynamic Enterprise Modeling
b. Contingency theory
c. Micromanagement
d. Logistics management

29. _____ is the level of inventory that minimizes the total inventory holding costs and ordering costs. The framework used to determine this order quantity is also known as Wilson _____ Model. The model was developed by F. W. Harris in 1913.

a. Event management
b. Anti-leadership
c. Effective executive
d. Economic order quantity

Chapter 5. MANUFACTURING- AND SERVICE-MANAGEMENT BEST PRACTICES

30. _____ refers to the structured transmission of data between organizations by electronic means. It is used to transfer electronic documents from one computer system to another (ie) from one trading partner to another trading partner. It is more than mere E-mail; for instance, organizations might replace bills of lading and even checks with appropriate _____ messages.
   a. AAAI
   b. A Stake in the Outcome
   c. Electronic data interchange
   d. A4e

31. A _____ is the system of organizations, people, technology, activities, information and resources involved in moving a product or service from supplier to customer. _____ activities transform natural resources, raw materials and components into a finished product that is delivered to the end customer. In sophisticated _____ systems, used products may re-enter the _____ at any point where residual value is recyclable.
   a. Wholesalers
   b. Packaging
   c. Drop shipping
   d. Supply chain

32. _____ is the management of a network of interconnected businesses involved in the ultimate provision of product and service packages required by end customers (Harland, 1996.) _____ spans all movement and storage of raw materials, work-in-process inventory, and finished goods from point of origin to point of consumption (supply chain.)

The definition an American professional association put forward is that _____ encompasses the planning and management of all activities involved in sourcing, procurement, conversion, and logistics management activities.

   a. Drop shipping
   b. Freight forwarder
   c. Packaging
   d. Supply chain management

33. In decision theory and estimation theory, the _____ of an estimator, $\hat{\theta}$, of an unknown parameter of the distribution, θ, is the expected value of the loss function

$$R(\theta, \hat{\theta}) = \mathbb{E}_\theta L(\theta, \hat{\theta}) = \int L(\theta, \hat{\theta})\, dP_\theta.$$

where dP_θ is a probability measure parametrized by θ.

- For a scalar parameter θ and a quadratic loss function,

$$L(\theta, \hat{\theta}) = (\theta - \hat{\theta})^2$$

the _____ function becomes the mean squared error of the estimate,

$$R(\theta, \hat{\theta}) = E_\theta (\theta - \hat{\theta})^2$$

- In density estimation, the unknown parameter is probability density itself. The loss function is typically chosen to be a norm in an appropriate function space. For example, for L^2 norm,

$$L(f, \hat{f}) = \|f - \hat{f}\|_2^2$$

the _____ function becomes the mean integrated squared error

$$R(f, \hat{f}) = E\|f - \hat{f}\|^2$$

    a. Linear model   b. Risk aversion
    c. Financial modeling   d. Risk

34. In accounting and auditing, _____ is defined as a process effected by an organization's structure, work and authority flows, people and management information systems, designed to help the organization accomplish specific goals or objectives. It is a means by which an organization's resources are directed, monitored, and measured. It plays an important role in preventing and detecting fraud and protecting the organization's resources, both physical (e.g., machinery and property) and intangible (e.g., reputation or intellectual property such as trademarks.)
    a. Audit committee   b. Internal auditing
    c. A Stake in the Outcome   d. Internal control

35. A _____ is a list of the general tasks and responsibilities of a position. Typically, it also includes to whom the position reports, specifications such as the qualifications needed by the person in the job, salary range for the position, etc. A _____ is usually developed by conducting a job analysis, which includes examining the tasks and sequences of tasks necessary to perform the job.
    a. Recruitment advertising   b. Recruitment
    c. Job description   d. Recruitment Process Insourcing

36. _____ is the provision of service to customers before, during and after a purchase.

According to Turban et al. (2002), '_____ is a series of activities designed to enhance the level of customer satisfaction - that is, the feeling that a product or service has met the customer expectation.'

Chapter 5. MANUFACTURING- AND SERVICE-MANAGEMENT BEST PRACTICES

Its importance varies by product, industry and customer; defective or broken merchandise can be exchanged, often only with a receipt and within a specified time frame.

a. 28-hour day
b. Service rate
c. 1990 Clean Air Act
d. Customer service

37. The phrase mergers and _____s refers to the aspect of corporate strategy, corporate finance and management dealing with the buying, selling and combining of different companies that can aid, finance, or help a growing company in a given industry grow rapidly without having to create another business entity.

An _____, also known as a takeover or a buyout, is the buying of one company (the 'target') by another. An _____ may be friendly or hostile.

a. A Stake in the Outcome
b. AAAI
c. A4e
d. Acquisition

38. A _____ is a relatively new executive level position at a corporation, company, organization typically reporting directly to the CEO or board of directors. The _____ is responsible for a brand's image, experience, and promise, and propagating it throughout all aspects of the company. The brand officer oversees marketing, advertising, design, public relations and customer service departments.

a. Chief executive officer
b. Chief brand officer
c. Purchasing manager
d. Director of communications

39. The _____ of 2002 (Pub.L. 107-204, 116 Stat. 745, enacted July 30, 2002), also known as the Public Company Accounting Reform and Investor Protection Act of 2002 and commonly called Sarbanes-Oxley, Sarbox or SOX, is a United States federal law enacted on July 30, 2002, as a reaction to a number of major corporate and accounting scandals including those affecting Enron, Tyco International, Adelphia, Peregrine Systems and WorldCom.

a. Fair Labor Standards Act
b. Letter of credit
c. Sarbanes-Oxley Act
d. Sarbanes-Oxley Act of 2002

40. The _____, first published in 1952, is one of a number of uniform acts that have been promulgated in conjunction with efforts to harmonize the law of sales and other commercial transactions in all 50 states within the United States of America. This objective is deemed important because of the prevalence of commercial transactions that extend beyond one state (for example, where the goods are manufactured in state A, warehoused in state B, sold from state C and delivered in state D.) The _____ deals primarily with transactions involving personal property (movable property), not real property (immovable property.)

a. A4e
b. AAAI
c. A Stake in the Outcome
d. Uniform Commercial Code

41. The _____ of 1977 (15 U.S.C. §§ 78dd-1, et seq.) is a United States federal law known primarily for two of its main provisions, one that addresses accounting transparency requirements under the Securities Exchange Act of 1934 and another concerning bribery of foreign officials.

a. Foreign Corrupt Practices Act
b. Social Security Act of 1965
c. Meritor Savings Bank v. Vinson
d. Limited liability

Chapter 5. MANUFACTURING- AND SERVICE-MANAGEMENT BEST PRACTICES

42. _____ is a cross-disciplinary area concerned with protecting the safety, health and welfare of people engaged in work or employment. The goal of all _____ programs is to foster a work free safe environment. As a secondary effect, it may also protect co-workers, family members, employers, customers, suppliers, nearby communities, and other members of the public who are impacted by the workplace environment.
 a. Occupational Safety and Health
 b. A Stake in the Outcome
 c. AAAI
 d. A4e

43. The _____ is the primary federal law which governs occupational health and safety in the private sector and federal government in the United States. It was enacted by Congress in 1970 and was signed by President Richard Nixon on December 29, 1970. Its main goal is to ensure that employers provide employees with an environment free from recognized hazards, such as exposure to toxic chemicals, excessive noise levels, mechanical dangers, heat or cold stress, or unsanitary conditions.
 a. United States Department of Justice
 b. Unemployment Action Center
 c. Unemployment and Farm Relief Act
 d. Occupational Safety and Health Act

44. A _____ is typically described as a deliberate plan of action to guide decisions and achieve rational outcome(s.) However, the term may also be used to denote what is actually done, even though it is unplanned.

The term may apply to government, private sector organizations and groups, and individuals.

 a. 33 Strategies of War
 b. 1990 Clean Air Act
 c. Policy
 d. 28-hour day

45. _____ is a graphic tool for defining the relationship between customer desires and the firm/product capabilities. It is a part of the Quality Function Deployment (QFD) and it utilizes a planning matrix to relate what the customer wants to how a firm (that produce the products) is going to meet those wants. It looks like a House with correlation matrix as its roof, customer wants versus product features as the main part, competitor evaluation as the porch etc.
 a. Decision Matrix
 b. Consensus-seeking decision-making
 c. House of quality
 d. Health management system

46. _____ is a business management strategy aimed at embedding awareness of quality in all organizational processes. _____ has been widely used in manufacturing, education, hospitals, call centers, government, and service industries, as well as NASA space and science programs.

As defined by the International Organization for Standardization (ISO):

 '_____ is a management approach for an organization, centered on quality, based on the participation of all its members and aiming at long-term success through customer satisfaction, and benefits to all members of the organization and to society.' ISO 8402:1994

One major aim is to reduce variation from every process so that greater consistency of effort is obtained. (Royse, D., Thyer, B., Padgett D., ' Logan T., 2006)

 a. Total quality management
 b. 1990 Clean Air Act
 c. 28-hour day
 d. Quality management

Chapter 5. MANUFACTURING- AND SERVICE-MANAGEMENT BEST PRACTICES

47. _____ is a separate and emerging business-process management methodology related to traditional Six Sigma. While the tools and order used in Six Sigma require a process to be in place and functioning, _____ has the objective of determining the needs of customers and the business, and driving those needs into the product solution so created. _____ is relevant to the complex system/product synthesis phase, especially in the context of unprecedented system development.
   a. 1990 Clean Air Act
   b. Design for Six Sigma
   c. 28-hour day
   d. Design methods

48. The _____ is a not-for-profit United States association for the benefit of the purchasing and supply management profession, particularly in the areas of education and research.

It was founded in 1913 as the New York Association of Purchasing Management after a purchasing meeting organized by the Thomas Register. It was established in 1915 as the National Association of Purchasing Management.

   a. Institute for Supply Management
   b. A4e
   c. AAAI
   d. A Stake in the Outcome

49. A _____ is a set of instructions having the force of a directive, covering those features of operations that lend themselves to a definite or standardized procedure without loss of effectiveness. Standard Operating Policies and Procedures can be effective catalysts to drive performance improvement and improving organizational results.
   a. 1990 Clean Air Act
   b. Longitudinal study
   c. Risk-benefit analysis
   d. Standard operating procedure

Chapter 6. MARKETING- AND SALES-MANAGEMENT BEST PRACTICES

1. _____ is a corporate title referring to an executive responsible for various marketing in an organization. Most often the position reports to the chief executive officer.

With primary or shared responsibility for areas such as sales management, product development, distribution channel management, public relations, marketing communications (including advertising and promotions), pricing, market research, and customer service, _____s are faced with a diverse range of specialized disciplines in which they are forced to be knowledgeable.

   a. Small and medium enterprises
   b. Food Marketing Institute
   c. Business Roundtable
   d. Chief marketing officer

2. _____ is an integrated communications-based process through which individuals and communities discover that existing and newly-identified needs and wants may be satisfied by the products and services of others.

_____ is defined by the American _____ Association as the activity, set of institutions, and processes for creating, communicating, delivering, and exchanging offerings that have value for customers, clients, partners, and society at large. The term developed from the original meaning which referred literally to going to market, as in shopping, or going to a market to buy or sell goods or services.

   a. Market development
   b. Marketing
   c. Customer relationship management
   d. Disruptive technology

3. A _____ is a group of people or organizations sharing one or more characteristics that cause them to have similar product and/or service needs. A true _____ meets all of the following criteria: it is distinct from other segments (different segments have different needs), it is homogeneous within the segment (exhibits common needs); it responds similarly to a market stimulus, and it can be reached by a market intervention. The term is also used when consumers with identical product and/or service needs are divided up into groups so they can be charged different amounts.
   a. SWOT analysis
   b. Context analysis
   c. Customer relationship management
   d. Market segment

4. A _____ is a name or trademark connected with a product or producer. _____s have become increasingly important components of culture and the economy, now being described as 'cultural accessories and personal philosophies'.

Some people distinguish the psychological aspect of a _____ from the experiential aspect.

   a. Brand
   b. Brand loyalty
   c. Brand extension
   d. Brand awareness

5. _____ is the application of marketing techniques to a specific product, product line, or brand. It seeks to increase the product's perceived value to the customer and thereby increase brand franchise and brand equity. Marketers see a brand as an implied promise that the level of quality people have come to expect from a brand will continue with future purchases of the same product.
   a. Brand names
   b. Brand extension
   c. Brand management
   d. Brand loyalty

6. _____ is, in very basic words, a position a firm occupies against its competitors.

Chapter 6. MARKETING- AND SALES-MANAGEMENT BEST PRACTICES

According to Michael Porter, the three methods for creating a sustainable _____ are through:

1. Cost leadership

2. Differentiation

3. Focus (economics)

   a. Theory Z   b. 1990 Clean Air Act
   c. 28-hour day   d. Competitive advantage

7. In business, operating margin, operating income margin, operating profit margin or _____ is the ratio of operating income (operating profit in the UK) divided by net sales, usually presented in percent.

(Relevant figures in italics)

It is a measurement of what proportion of a company's revenue is left over, before taxes and other indirect costs (such as rent, bonus, interest, etc.), after paying for variable costs of production as wages, raw materials, etc. A good operating margin is needed for a company to be able to pay for its fixed costs, such as interest on debt.

   a. P/E ratio   b. Return on sales
   c. Return on equity   d. Rate of return

8. _____ is a strategic planning method used to evaluate the Strengths, Weaknesses, Opportunities, and Threats involved in a project or in a business venture. It involves specifying the objective of the business venture or project and identifying the internal and external factors that are favorable and unfavorable to achieving that objective. The technique is credited to Albert Humphrey, who led a convention at Stanford University in the 1960s and 1970s using data from Fortune 500 companies.

   a. Corporate image   b. SWOT analysis
   c. Marketing   d. Market share

9. _____ is a term used in business and Information Technology (through ITIL) to describe the process of capturing a customer's requirements. Specifically, the _____ is a market research technique that produces a detailed set of customer wants and needs, organized into a hierarchical structure, and then prioritized in terms of relative importance and satisfaction with current alternatives. _____ studies typically consist of both qualitative and quantitative research steps.

   a. Board of governors   b. Goal setting
   c. Voice of the customer   d. Business philosophy

Chapter 6. MARKETING- AND SALES-MANAGEMENT BEST PRACTICES

10. _____ is one of the managerial functions like planning, organizing, staffing and directing. It is an important function because it helps to check the errors and to take the corrective action so that deviation from standards are minimized and stated goals of the organization are achieved in desired manner. According to modern concepts, _____ is a foreseeing action whereas earlier concept of _____ was used only when errors were detected. _____ in management means setting standards, measuring actual performance and taking corrective action.

- a. Control
- b. Schedule of reinforcement
- c. Turnover
- d. Decision tree pruning

11. In accounting and auditing, _____ is defined as a process effected by an organization's structure, work and authority flows, people and management information systems, designed to help the organization accomplish specific goals or objectives. It is a means by which an organization's resources are directed, monitored, and measured. It plays an important role in preventing and detecting fraud and protecting the organization's resources, both physical (e.g., machinery and property) and intangible (e.g., reputation or intellectual property such as trademarks.)

- a. Audit committee
- b. Internal control
- c. Internal auditing
- d. A Stake in the Outcome

12. _____s (or MarCom or Integrated _____s) are messages and related media used to communicate with a market. Those who practice advertising, branding, direct marketing, graphic design, marketing, packaging, promotion, publicity, sponsorship, public relations, sales, sales promotion and online marketing are termed marketing communicators, _____ managers, or more briefly as marcom managers.

Traditionally, _____ practitioners focus on the creation and execution of printed marketing collateral; however, academic and professional research developed the practice to use strategic elements of branding and marketing in order to ensure consistency of message delivery throughout an organization.

- a. Marketing communication
- b. Thomas Dale DeLay
- c. Adam Smith
- d. Abraham Harold Maslow

13. _____ can be considered to have three main components: quality control, quality assurance and quality improvement. _____ is focused not only on product quality, but also the means to achieve it. _____ therefore uses quality assurance and control of processes as well as products to achieve more consistent quality.

- a. 28-hour day
- b. 1990 Clean Air Act
- c. Quality management
- d. Total quality management

14. The general definition of an _____ is an evaluation of a person, organization, system, process, project or product. _____s are performed to ascertain the validity and reliability of information; also to provide an assessment of a system's internal control. The goal of an _____ is to express an opinion on the person / organization/system (etc) in question, under evaluation based on work done on a test basis.

- a. Internal control
- b. A Stake in the Outcome
- c. Audit committee
- d. Audit

Chapter 6. MARKETING- AND SALES-MANAGEMENT BEST PRACTICES

15. A _____ is a volunteer group composed of workers (or even students), usually under the leadership of their supervisor (but they can elect a team leader), who are trained to identify, analyse and solve work-related problems and present their solutions to management in order to improve the performance of the organization, and motivate and enrich the work of employees. When matured, true _____s become self-managing, having gained the confidence of management. _____s are an alternative to the dehumanising concept of the Division of Labour, where workers or individuals are treated like robots.

a. Connectionist expert systems
b. Certified in Production and Inventory Management
c. Competency-based job descriptions
d. Quality circle

16. A _____ or business method is a collection of related, structured activities or tasks that produce a specific service or product (serve a particular goal) for a particular customer or customers. It often can be visualized with a flowchart as a sequence of activities.

There are three types of _____es:

1. Management processes, the processes that govern the operation of a system. Typical management processes include 'Corporate Governance' and 'Strategic Management'.
2. Operational processes, processes that constitute the core business and create the primary value stream. Typical operational processes are Purchasing, Manufacturing, Marketing, and Sales.
3. Supporting processes, which support the core processes. Examples include Accounting, Recruitment, Technical support.

A _____ begins with a customer's need and ends with a customer's need fulfillment. Process oriented organizations break down the barriers of structural departments and try to avoid functional silos.

a. 1990 Clean Air Act
b. 33 Strategies of War
c. Business process
d. 28-hour day

17. The loyalty business model is a business model used in strategic management in which company resources are employed so as to increase the loyalty of customers and other stakeholders in the expectation that corporate objectives will be met or surpassed. A typical example of this type of model is: quality of product or service leads to customer satisfaction, which leads to _____, which leads to profitability.

Fredrick Reichheld (1996) expanded the loyalty business model beyond customers and employees.

a. 28-hour day
b. 1990 Clean Air Act
c. 33 Strategies of War
d. Customer loyalty

18. In decision theory and estimation theory, the _____ of an estimator, $\hat{\theta}$, of an unknown parameter of the distribution, θ, is the expected value of the loss function

$$R(\theta, \hat{\theta}) = \mathbb{E}_\theta L(\theta, \hat{\theta}) = \int L(\theta, \hat{\theta}) \, dP_\theta.$$

where dP_θ is a probability measure parametrized by θ.

- For a scalar parameter θ and a quadratic loss function,

$$L(\theta, \hat{\theta}) = (\theta - \hat{\theta})^2$$

the _____ function becomes the mean squared error of the estimate,

$$R(\theta, \hat{\theta}) = E_\theta (\theta - \hat{\theta})^2$$

- In density estimation, the unknown parameter is probability density itself. The loss function is typically chosen to be a norm in an appropriate function space. For example, for L^2 norm,

$$L(f, \hat{f}) = \|f - \hat{f}\|_2^2$$

the _____ function becomes the mean integrated squared error

$$R(f, \hat{f}) = E\|f - \hat{f}\|^2$$

    a. Linear model   b. Risk
    c. Risk aversion   d. Financial modeling

19. _____ is the identification, assessment, and prioritization of risks followed by coordinated and economical application of resources to minimize, monitor, and control the probability and/or impact of unfortunate events.. Risks can come from uncertainty in financial markets, project failures, legal liabilities, credit risk, accidents, natural causes and disasters as well as deliberate attacks from an adversary. Several _____ standards have been developed including the Project Management Institute, the National Institute of Science and Technology, actuarial societies, and ISO standards.
    a. Risk management   b. Succession planning
    c. Trademark   d. Kanban

20. A _____ is the system of organizations, people, technology, activities, information and resources involved in moving a product or service from supplier to customer. _____ activities transform natural resources, raw materials and components into a finished product that is delivered to the end customer. In sophisticated _____ systems, used products may re-enter the _____ at any point where residual value is recyclable.
    a. Packaging   b. Supply chain
    c. Drop shipping   d. Wholesalers

21. _____ is the management of a network of interconnected businesses involved in the ultimate provision of product and service packages required by end customers (Harland, 1996.) _____ spans all movement and storage of raw materials, work-in-process inventory, and finished goods from point of origin to point of consumption (supply chain.)

Chapter 6. MARKETING- AND SALES-MANAGEMENT BEST PRACTICES

The definition an American professional association put forward is that _____ encompasses the planning and management of all activities involved in sourcing, procurement, conversion, and logistics management activities.

a. Freight forwarder
b. Supply chain management
c. Drop shipping
d. Packaging

22. In a publicly-held company, an _____ is an operating committee of the Board of Directors, typically charged with oversight of financial reporting and disclosure. Committee members are drawn from members of the Company's board of directors, with a Chairperson selected from among the members. An _____ of a publicly-traded company in the United States is composed of independent and outside directors referred to as non-executive directors, at least one of which is typically a financial expert.

a. Internal auditing
b. A Stake in the Outcome
c. Internal control
d. Audit committee

23. Marketing research is a form of business research and is generally divided into two categories: consumer _____ and business-to-business (B2B) _____, which was previously known as industrial marketing research. Consumer marketing research studies the buying habits of individual people while business-to-business marketing research investigates the markets for products sold by one business to another.

Consumer _____ is a form of applied sociology that concentrates on understanding the behaviours, whims and preferences, of consumers in a market-based economy, and aims to understand the effects and comparative success of marketing campaigns.

a. Mystery shoppers
b. Market research
c. Questionnaire
d. Questionnaire construction

24. _____ consists of the processes a company uses to track and organize its contacts with its current and prospective customers. _____ software is used to support these processes; information about customers and customer interactions can be entered, stored and accessed by employees in different company departments. Typical _____ goals are to improve services provided to customers, and to use customer contact information for targeted marketing.

a. Customer relationship management
b. Green marketing
c. Disruptive technology
d. Marketing plan

25. The phrase _____, according to the Organization for Economic Co-operation and Development, refers to 'creative work undertaken on a systematic basis in order to increase the stock of knowledge, including knowledge of man, culture and society, and the use of this stock of knowledge to devise new applications [sic]'

New product design and development is more than often a crucial factor in the survival of a company. In an industry that is fast changing, firms must continually revise their design and range of products. This is necessary due to continuous technology change and development as well as other competitors and the changing preference of customers.

Chapter 6. MARKETING- AND SALES-MANAGEMENT BEST PRACTICES

a. Research and development
b. 33 Strategies of War
c. 28-hour day
d. 1990 Clean Air Act

26. An _____ is a body that advises the board of directors and management of a corporation but does not have authority to vote on corporate matters, nor a legal fiduciary responsibility.

a. Advisory board
b. Individual development planning
c. A Stake in the Outcome
d. A4e

27. The _____ of 1914, (October 151914, ch. 323, 38 Stat. 730, codified at 15 U.S.C. § 12-27, 29 U.S.C. § 52-53), was enacted in the United States to add further substance to the U.S. antitrust law regime by seeking to prevent anticompetitive practices in their incipiency. That regime started with the Sherman Antitrust Act of 1890, the first Federal law outlawing practices considered harmful to consumers (monopolies and cartels). The Clayton act specified particular prohibited conduct, the three-level enforcement scheme, the exemptions, and the remedial measures.

a. Long Service Leave
b. Legal working age
c. Munn v. Illinois
d. Clayton Antitrust Act

28. _____ is one of the four Ps of the marketing mix. The other three aspects are product, promotion, and place. It is also a key variable in microeconomic price allocation theory.

a. Pricing
b. Penetration pricing
c. Price floor
d. Transfer pricing

29. The _____ of 1936 (or Anti-Price Discrimination Act, 15 U.S.C. § 13) is a United States federal law that prohibits what were considered, at the time of passage, to be anticompetitive practices by producers, specifically price discrimination. It grew out of practices in which chain stores were allowed to purchase goods at lower prices than other retailers.

a. Robinson-Patman Act
b. Privity
c. Labor Management Reporting and Disclosure Act
d. Bona fide occupational qualification

30. _____ is an advertisement in which a particular product specifically mentions a competitor by name for the express purpose of showing why the competitor is inferior to the product naming it.

This should not be confused with parody advertisements, where a fictional product is being advertised for the purpose of poking fun at the particular advertisement, nor should it be confused with the use of a coined brand name for the purpose of comparing the product without actually naming an actual competitor. ('Wikipedia tastes better and is less filling than the Encyclopedia Galactica.')

In the 1980s, during what has been referred to as the cola wars, soft-drink manufacturer Pepsi ran a series of advertisements where people, caught on hidden camera, in a blind taste test, chose Pepsi over rival Coca-Cola.

a. 33 Strategies of War
b. 28-hour day
c. Comparative advertising
d. 1990 Clean Air Act

31. _____ is a term used in general business practice to describe methodologies, systems, and practices designed to generate new potential business clientele, generally operated through a variety of marketing techniques. _____ facilitates a business's connection between its outgoing consumer advertising and the responses to that advertising. These processes are designed for business-to-business and direct-to-consumer strategies.

Chapter 6. MARKETING- AND SALES-MANAGEMENT BEST PRACTICES   67

a. Request for Proposal
b. Lead generation
c. 1990 Clean Air Act
d. Lead management

32. The buzzwords _____ and viral advertising refer to marketing techniques that use pre-existing social networks to produce increases in brand awareness or to achieve other marketing objectives (such as product sales) through self-replicating viral processes, analogous to the spread of pathological and computer viruses. It can be word-of-mouth delivered or enhanced by the network effects of the Internet. Viral promotions may take the form of video clips, interactive Flash games, advergames, ebooks, brandable software, images, or even text messages.

a. 33 Strategies of War
b. Viral marketing
c. 1990 Clean Air Act
d. 28-hour day

33. _____ is a broad label that refers to any individuals or households that use goods and services generated within the economy. The concept of a _____ is used in different contexts, so that the usage and significance of the term may vary.

Typically when business people and economists talk of _____s they are talking about person as _____, an aggregated commodity item with little individuality other than that expressed in the buy/not-buy decision.

a. Consumer
b. 28-hour day
c. 1990 Clean Air Act
d. 33 Strategies of War

34. The United States federal wage garnishment law, widely known as the _____ guards employees from discharge by their employers because their wages have been garnished in any one week. It was approved by the government in 1968. The Wage and Hour Division of the United States Department of Labor includes the Employment Standards Administration, who administers the act.

a. 1990 Clean Air Act
b. 28-hour day
c. Consumer Credit Protection Act
d. Pure Food and Drug Act

35. The _____ is a US law that applies to labels on many consumer products. It requires the label to state:

- The identity of the product;
- The name and place of business of the manufacturer, packer, or distributor; and
- The net quantity of contents.

The contents statement must include both metric and U.S. customary units.

Passed under Lyndon B. Johnson in 1966, the law first took effect on July 1, 1967. The metric labeling requirement was added in 1992 and took effect on February 14, 1994.

a. 33 Strategies of War
b. 28-hour day
c. 1990 Clean Air Act
d. Fair Packaging and Labeling Act

36. The _____ of 1977 (15 U.S.C. §§ 78dd-1, et seq.) is a United States federal law known primarily for two of its main provisions, one that addresses accounting transparency requirements under the Securities Exchange Act of 1934 and another concerning bribery of foreign officials.

Chapter 6. MARKETING- AND SALES-MANAGEMENT BEST PRACTICES

a. Limited liability
b. Meritor Savings Bank v. Vinson
c. Social Security Act of 1965
d. Foreign Corrupt Practices Act

37. _____ is the science, art and technology of enclosing or protecting products for distribution, storage, sale, and use. _____ also refers to the process of design, evaluation, and production of packages. _____ can be described as a coordinated system of preparing goods for transport, warehousing, logistics, sale, and end use.
   a. Supply chain
   b. Wholesalers
   c. Packaging
   d. Supply chain management

38. The _____ was enacted in 1972 by the United States Congress. It established the United States Consumer Product Safety Commission as an independent agency of the United States federal government and defined its basic authority. The act gives CPSC the power to develop safety standards and pursue recalls for products that present unreasonable or substantial risks of injury or death to consumers.
   a. 28-hour day
   b. 1990 Clean Air Act
   c. 33 Strategies of War
   d. Consumer Product Safety Act

39. The _____ is an independent agency of the United States government, established in 1914 by the _____ Act. Its principal mission is the promotion of 'consumer protection' and the elimination and prevention of what regulators perceive to be harmfully 'anti-competitive' business practices, such as coercive monopoly.

The _____ Act was one of President Wilson's major acts against trusts.

   a. 28-hour day
   b. 33 Strategies of War
   c. 1990 Clean Air Act
   d. Federal Trade Commission

40. The _____ of 1914 (15 U.S.C Â§Â§ 41-58, as amended) established the Federal Trade Commission (FTC), a bipartisan body of five members appointed by the President of the United States for seven year terms. This Commission was authorized to issue Cease and Desist orders to large corporations to curb unfair trade practices. This Act also gave more flexibility to the US congress for judicial matters.
   a. Sarbanes-Oxley Act of 2002
   b. Federal Trade Commission Act
   c. Resource Conservation and Recovery Act
   d. Comprehensive Environmental Response, Compensation, and Liability Act

41. The _____ requires the Federal government to investigate and pursue trusts, companies and organizations suspected of violating the Act. It was the first United States Federal statute to limit cartels and monopolies, and today still forms the basis for most antitrust litigation by the federal government.
   a. Sherman Antitrust Act
   b. 33 Strategies of War
   c. 1990 Clean Air Act
   d. 28-hour day

42. The _____ of 1938 is a United States federal law that amended the Federal Trade Commission Act to add the clause 'unfair or deceptive acts or practices in commerce are hereby declared unlawful' to the Section 5 prohibition of unfair methods of competition, in order to protect consumers as well as competition.

1938 amendment to the federal trade commission act that authorized the FTC to restrict unfair or deceptive acts; also called the advertising act. Until this amendment was passed, the FTC could only restrict practices that were unfair to competitors.

Chapter 6. MARKETING- AND SALES-MANAGEMENT BEST PRACTICES

a. Drug test
c. Reverification
b. Financial Security Law of France
d. Wheeler-Lea Act

43. _____ is a concept in ethics with several meanings. It is often used synonymously with such concepts as responsibility, answerability, enforcement, blameworthiness, liability and other terms associated with the expectation of account-giving. As an aspect of governance, it has been central to discussions related to problems in both the public and private (corporation) worlds.
    a. Usury
    c. A4e
    b. A Stake in the Outcome
    d. Accountability

44. The _____ is an Act of the 106th United States Congress which repealed part of the Glass-Steagall Act of 1933, opening up competition among banks, securities companies and insurance companies.
    a. 33 Strategies of War
    c. 1990 Clean Air Act
    b. 28-hour day
    d. Gramm-Leach-Bliley Act

45. _____ are legal property rights over creations of the mind, both artistic and commercial, and the corresponding fields of law. Under _____ law, owners are granted certain exclusive rights to a variety of intangible assets, such as musical, literary, and artistic works; ideas, discoveries and inventions; and words, phrases, symbols, and designs. Common types of _____ include copyrights, trademarks, patents, industrial design rights and trade secrets.
    a. Intellectual property
    c. Equal Pay Act
    b. Intent
    d. Unemployment Action Center

46. _____ plant, and equipment, is a term used in accountancy for assets and property which cannot easily be converted into cash. This can be compared with current assets such as cash or bank accounts, which are described as liquid assets. In most cases, only tangible assets are referred to as fixed.
    a. Fixed asset
    c. 1990 Clean Air Act
    b. 33 Strategies of War
    d. 28-hour day

47. A _____ is a distinctive sign or indicator used by an individual, business organization, or other legal entity to identify that the products and/or services to consumers with which the _____ appears originate from a unique source and to distinguish its products or services from those of other entities.
    a. Trademark
    c. Virtual team
    b. Kanban
    d. Succession planning

Chapter 7. QUALITY-MANAGEMENT BEST PRACTICES

1. The _____ is given by the United States National Institute of Standards and Technology. Through the actions of the National Productivity Advisory Committee chaired by Jack Grayson, it was established by the Malcolm Baldrige National Quality Improvement Act of 1987 - Public Law 100-107 and named for Malcolm Baldrige, who served as United States Secretary of Commerce during the Reagan administration from 1981 until his 1987 death in a rodeo accident. APQC, , organized the first White House Conference on Productivity, spearheading the creation and design of the _____ in 1987, and jointly administering the award for its first three years.

   a. Malcolm Baldrige National Quality Award   b. Business Network Transformation
   c. Time and attendance   d. Scenario planning

2. _____ can be considered to have three main components: quality control, quality assurance and quality improvement. _____ is focused not only on product quality, but also the means to achieve it. _____ therefore uses quality assurance and control of processes as well as products to achieve more consistent quality.

   a. 28-hour day   b. 1990 Clean Air Act
   c. Total quality management   d. Quality management

3. _____ is an organization's process of defining its strategy and making decisions on allocating its resources to pursue this strategy, including its capital and people. Various business analysis techniques can be used in _____, including SWOT analysis (Strengths, Weaknesses, Opportunities, and Threats) and PEST analysis (Political, Economic, Social, and Technological analysis) or STEER analysis involving Socio-cultural, Technological, Economic, Ecological, and Regulatory factors and EPISTEL (Environment, Political, Informatic, Social, Technological, Economic and Legal)

_____ is the formal consideration of an organization's future course. All _____ deals with at least one of three key questions:

1. 'What do we do?'
2. 'For whom do we do it?'
3. 'How do we excel?'

In business _____, the third question is better phrased 'How can we beat or avoid competition?'. (Bradford and Duncan, page 1.)

   a. Strategic planning   b. 28-hour day
   c. 1990 Clean Air Act   d. 33 Strategies of War

4. _____ is a business management strategy aimed at embedding awareness of quality in all organizational processes. _____ has been widely used in manufacturing, education, hospitals, call centers, government, and service industries, as well as NASA space and science programs.

As defined by the International Organization for Standardization (ISO):

> '_____ is a management approach for an organization, centered on quality, based on the participation of all its members and aiming at long-term success through customer satisfaction, and benefits to all members of the organization and to society.' ISO 8402:1994

One major aim is to reduce variation from every process so that greater consistency of effort is obtained. (Royse, D., Thyer, B., Padgett D., ' Logan T., 2006)

Chapter 7. QUALITY-MANAGEMENT BEST PRACTICES

a. 28-hour day
b. Total quality management
c. Quality management
d. 1990 Clean Air Act

5. The general definition of an _____ is an evaluation of a person, organization, system, process, project or product. _____s are performed to ascertain the validity and reliability of information; also to provide an assessment of a system's internal control. The goal of an _____ is to express an opinion on the person / organization/system (etc) in question, under evaluation based on work done on a test basis.

a. Audit committee
b. Internal control
c. A Stake in the Outcome
d. Audit

6. A _____ or business method is a collection of related, structured activities or tasks that produce a specific service or product (serve a particular goal) for a particular customer or customers. It often can be visualized with a flowchart as a sequence of activities.

There are three types of _____ es:

1. Management processes, the processes that govern the operation of a system. Typical management processes include 'Corporate Governance' and 'Strategic Management'.
2. Operational processes, processes that constitute the core business and create the primary value stream. Typical operational processes are Purchasing, Manufacturing, Marketing, and Sales.
3. Supporting processes, which support the core processes. Examples include Accounting, Recruitment, Technical support.

A _____ begins with a customer's need and ends with a customer's need fulfillment. Process oriented organizations break down the barriers of structural departments and try to avoid functional silos.

a. 33 Strategies of War
b. 28-hour day
c. 1990 Clean Air Act
d. Business process

7. _____ is one of the managerial functions like planning, organizing, staffing and directing. It is an important function because it helps to check the errors and to take the corrective action so that deviation from standards are minimized and stated goals of the organization are achieved in desired manner. According to modern concepts, _____ is a foreseeing action whereas earlier concept of _____ was used only when errors were detected. _____ in management means setting standards, measuring actual performance and taking corrective action.

a. Decision tree pruning
b. Schedule of reinforcement
c. Control
d. Turnover

Chapter 7. QUALITY-MANAGEMENT BEST PRACTICES

8. _____ is an increasingly broadening term with which an organization, or other human system describes the combination of traditionally administrative personnel functions with acquisition and application of skills, knowledge and experience, Employee Relations and resource planning at various levels. The field draws upon concepts developed in Industrial/Organizational Psychology and System Theory. _____ has at least two related interpretations depending on context. The original usage derives from political economy and economics, where it was traditionally called labor, one of four factors of production although this perspective is changing as a function of new and ongoing research into more strategic approaches at national levels. This first usage is used more in terms of '_____ development', and can go beyond just organizations to the level of nations . The more traditional usage within corporations and businesses refers to the individuals within a firm or agency, and to the portion of the organization that deals with hiring, firing, training, and other personnel issues, typically referred to as `_____ management'.
   a. Human resources
   b. Progressive discipline
   c. Human resource management
   d. Bradford Factor

9. _____ is a process of planning and controlling the performance or execution of any type of activity, such as:

   - a project (project _____) or
   - a process (process _____, sometimes referred to as the process performance measurement and management system.)

   Organization's senior management is responsible for carrying out its _____.

   a. Human Relations Movement
   b. Work design
   c. Participatory management
   d. Management Process

10. _____ refers to planned and systematic production processes that provide confidence in a product's suitability for its intended purpose. Refer to the definition by Merriam-Webster for further information . It is a set of activities intended to ensure that products (goods and/or services) satisfy customer requirements in a systematic, reliable fashion.
    a. Risk assessment
    b. 1990 Clean Air Act
    c. 28-hour day
    d. Quality assurance

11. A _____ is a volunteer group composed of workers (or even students), usually under the leadership of their supervisor (but they can elect a team leader), who are trained to identify, analyse and solve work-related problems and present their solutions to management in order to improve the performance of the organization, and motivate and enrich the work of employees. When matured, true _____s become self-managing, having gained the confidence of management.
    _____s are an alternative to the dehumanising concept of the Division of Labour, where workers or individuals are treated like robots.
    a. Certified in Production and Inventory Management
    b. Competency-based job descriptions
    c. Connectionist expert systems
    d. Quality circle

12. In engineering and manufacturing, _____ and quality engineering are used in developing systems to ensure products or services are designed and produced to meet or exceed customer requirements. Refer to the definition by Merriam-Webster for further information . These systems are often developed in conjunction with other business and engineering disciplines using a cross-functional approach.
    a. Statistical process control
    b. Process capability
    c. Single Minute Exchange of Die
    d. Quality control

Chapter 7. QUALITY-MANAGEMENT BEST PRACTICES 73

13. _____ ('Plan-Do-Check-Act') is an iterative four-step problem-solving process typically used in business process improvement. It is also known as the Deming Cycle, Shewhart cycle, Deming Wheel, or Plan-Do-Study-Act.

_____ was made popular by Dr. W. Edwards Deming, who is considered by many to be the father of modern quality control; however it was always referred to by him as the Shewhart cycle. Later in Deming's career, he modified _____ to Plan, Do, Study, Act (PDSA) so as to better describe his recommendations.

- a. Decentralization
- b. Management by exception
- c. PDCA
- d. Management team

14. _____ refers to the movement of cash into or out of a business or financial product. It is usually measured during a specified, finite period of time. Measurement of _____ can be used

- to determine a project's rate of return or value. The time of _____s into and out of projects are used as inputs in financial models such as internal rate of return, and net present value.
- to determine problems with a business's liquidity. Being profitable does not necessarily mean being liquid. A company can fail because of a shortage of cash, even while profitable.
- as an alternate measure of a business's profits when it is believed that accrual accounting concepts do not represent economic realities. For example, a company may be notionally profitable but generating little operational cash (as may be the case for a company that barters its products rather than selling for cash.) In such a case, the company may be deriving additional operating cash by issuing shares evaluating default risk, re-investment requirements, etc.

_____ is a generic term used differently depending on the context. It may be defined by users for their own purposes.

- a. Gross profit
- b. Cash flow
- c. Sweat equity
- d. Gross profit margin

15. _____ is the discipline of planning, organizing and managing resources to bring about the successful completion of specific project goals and objectives. It is often closely related to and sometimes conflated with Program management.

A project is a finite endeavor--having specific start and completion dates--undertaken to meet particular goals and objectives, usually to bring about beneficial change or added value.

- a. Work package
- b. Precedence diagram
- c. Project engineer
- d. Project management

16. _____, in strategic management and marketing is, according to Carlton O'Neal, the percentage or proportion of the total available market or market segment that is being serviced by a company. It can be expressed as a company's sales revenue (from that market) divided by the total sales revenue available in that market. It can also be expressed as a company's unit sales volume (in a market) divided by the total volume of units sold in that market.

- a. Green marketing
- b. Business-to-business
- c. Marketing plan
- d. Market share

17. The _____ percentage shows how profitable a company's assets are in generating revenue.

_____ can be computed as:

$$ROA = \frac{\text{Net Income} + \text{Interest Expense} - \text{Interest Tax savings}}{\text{Average Total Assets}}$$

This number tells you what the company can do with what it has, i.e. how many dollars of earnings they derive from each dollar of assets they control. Its a useful number for comparing competing companies in the same industry.

a. Return on Capital Employed
b. Return on equity
c. P/E ratio
d. Return on assets

18. In business, operating margin, operating income margin, operating profit margin or _____ is the ratio of operating income (operating profit in the UK) divided by net sales, usually presented in percent.

(Relevant figures in italics)

It is a measurement of what proportion of a company's revenue is left over, before taxes and other indirect costs (such as rent, bonus, interest, etc.), after paying for variable costs of production as wages, raw materials, etc. A good operating margin is needed for a company to be able to pay for its fixed costs, such as interest on debt.

a. Return on equity
b. Rate of return
c. P/E ratio
d. Return on sales

19. In business and accounting, _____s are everything of value that is owned by a person or company. Any property or object of value that one possesses, usually considered as applicable to the payment of one's debts is considered an _____. Simplistically stated, _____s are things of value that can be readily converted into cash.

a. Asset
b. AAAI
c. A Stake in the Outcome
d. A4e

20. _____ is a group creativity technique designed to generate a large number of ideas for the solution of a problem. The method was first popularized in the late 1930s by Alex Faickney Osborn in a book called Applied Imagination. Osborn proposed that groups could double their creative output with _____.

a. Brainstorming
b. Abraham Harold Maslow
c. Affiliation
d. Adam Smith

Chapter 7. QUALITY-MANAGEMENT BEST PRACTICES

21. In economics, business, retail, and accounting, a _____ is the value of money that has been used up to produce something, and hence is not available for use anymore. In economics, a _____ is an alternative that is given up as a result of a decision. In business, the _____ may be one of acquisition, in which case the amount of money expended to acquire it is counted as _____.

   a. Cost overrun
   c. Cost allocation
   b. Fixed costs
   d. Cost

22. A _____ is the belief that there is a technique, method, process, activity, incentive or reward that is more effective at delivering a particular outcome than any other technique, method, process, etc. The idea is that with proper processes, checks, and testing, a desired outcome can be delivered with fewer problems and unforeseen complications. _____s can also be defined as the most efficient (least amount of effort) and effective (best results) way of accomplishing a task, based on repeatable procedures that have proven themselves over time for large numbers of people.

   a. Fix it twice
   c. Hierarchical organization
   b. Design management
   d. Best practice

23. The concept of quality costs is a means to quantify the total _____-related efforts and deficiencies. It was first described by Armand V. Feigenbaum in a 1956 Harvard Business Review article.

Prior to its introduction, the general perception was that higher quality requires higher costs, either by buying better materials or machines or by hiring more labor.

   a. Quality costs
   c. Cost accounting
   b. Fixed costs
   d. Cost of quality

24. _____ is a business management strategy, initially implemented by Motorola, that today enjoys widespread application in many sectors of industry.

_____ seeks to improve the quality of process outputs by identifying and removing the causes of defects (errors) and variation in manufacturing and business processes. It uses a set of quality management methods, including statistical methods, and creates a special infrastructure of people within the organization ('Black Belts' etc.)

   a. Production line
   c. Takt time
   b. Theory of constraints
   d. Six Sigma

25. _____ is the provision of service to customers before, during and after a purchase.

According to Turban et al. (2002), '_____ is a series of activities designed to enhance the level of customer satisfaction - that is, the feeling that a product or service has met the customer expectation.'

Its importance varies by product, industry and customer; defective or broken merchandise can be exchanged, often only with a receipt and within a specified time frame.

   a. 1990 Clean Air Act
   c. Service rate
   b. 28-hour day
   d. Customer service

Chapter 7. QUALITY-MANAGEMENT BEST PRACTICES

26. A _____ or labor union is an organization of workers who have banded together to achieve common goals in key areas and working conditions. The _____, through its leadership, bargains with the employer on behalf of union members (rank and file members) and negotiates labor contracts (Collective bargaining) with employers. This may include the negotiation of wages, work rules, complaint procedures, rules governing hiring, firing and promotion of workers, benefits, workplace safety and policies.
   a. Labour law
   b. Working time
   c. Company union
   d. Trade union

27. A _____ or chief operations officer is a corporate officer responsible for managing the day-to-day activities of the corporation and for operations management (OM.) The _____ is one of the highest-ranking members of an organization's senior management, monitoring the daily operations of the company and reporting to the board of directors and the top executive officer, usually the chief executive officer (CEO.) The _____ is usually an executive or senior officer.
   a. Supervisory board
   b. Value based pricing
   c. Product innovation
   d. Chief operating officer

28. _____ is an advertisement in which a particular product specifically mentions a competitor by name for the express purpose of showing why the competitor is inferior to the product naming it.

This should not be confused with parody advertisements, where a fictional product is being advertised for the purpose of poking fun at the particular advertisement, nor should it be confused with the use of a coined brand name for the purpose of comparing the product without actually naming an actual competitor. ('Wikipedia tastes better and is less filling than the Encyclopedia Galactica.')

In the 1980s, during what has been referred to as the cola wars, soft-drink manufacturer Pepsi ran a series of advertisements where people, caught on hidden camera, in a blind taste test, chose Pepsi over rival Coca-Cola.

   a. 33 Strategies of War
   b. 28-hour day
   c. 1990 Clean Air Act
   d. Comparative advertising

29. In statistics, a _____ is a graphical display of tabulated frequencies, shown as bars. It shows what proportion of cases fall into each of several categories: it is a form of data binning. The categories are usually specified as non-overlapping intervals of some variable.
   a. Statistics
   b. Correlation
   c. Histogram
   d. Standard deviation

30. In corporate finance, _____ or _____ is an estimate of true economic profit after making corrective adjustments to GAAP accounting, including deducting the opportunity cost of equity capital. _____ can be measured as Net Operating Profit After Taxes(or NOPAT) less the money cost of capital. _____ is similar in nature to that of calculating another financial performance measure - Residual Income , however, there are a few complexities involved with coming up with the elements for calculating _____ over RI such as the myriad adjustments that might be made to NOPAT before it is suitable for the formula below.
   a. A Stake in the Outcome
   b. AAAI
   c. Economic value added
   d. A4e

31. A scatter plot is a type of display using Cartesian coordinates to display values for two variables for a set of data.

Chapter 7. QUALITY-MANAGEMENT BEST PRACTICES

The data is displayed as a collection of points, each having the value of one variable determining the position on the horizontal axis and the value of the other variable determining the position on the vertical axis. A scatter plot is also called a scatter chart, _____ and scatter graph.

- a. 33 Strategies of War
- b. 1990 Clean Air Act
- c. 28-hour day
- d. Scatter diagram

32. _____ refers to the difference between the cost of materials purchased by a company plus the cost of the labor to assemble a product and the price at which the company sells the product. An example is the price of gasoline at the pump over the price of the oil in it. In national accounts used in macroeconomics, it refers to the contribution of the factors of production, i.e., land, labor, and capital goods, to raising the value of a product and corresponds to the incomes received by the owners of these factors.

- a. Minimum wage
- b. Deregulation
- c. Rehn-Meidner Model
- d. Value added

33. The _____ in statistical process control is a tool used to determine whether a manufacturing or business process is in a state of statistical control or not.

If the chart indicates that the process is currently under control then it can be used with confidence to predict the future performance of the process. If the chart indicates that the process being monitored is not in control, the pattern it reveals can help determine the source of variation to be eliminated to bring the process back into control.

- a. Failure rate
- b. Control chart
- c. Time series analysis
- d. Simple moving average

34. A _____ is a common type of chart, that represents an algorithm or process, showing the steps as boxes of various kinds, and their order by connecting these with arrows. _____s are used in analyzing, designing, documenting or managing a process or program in various fields.

The first structured method for documenting process flow, the 'flow process chart', was introduced by Frank Gilbreth to members of ASME in 1921 as the presentation 'Process Charts--First Steps in Finding the One Best Way'.

- a. 28-hour day
- b. 1990 Clean Air Act
- c. 33 Strategies of War
- d. Flowchart

35. The _____, widely known as ISO , is an international-standard-setting body composed of representatives from various national standards organizations. Founded on 23 February 1947, the organization promulgates worldwide proprietary industrial and commercial standards. It is headquartered in Geneva, Switzerland.

- a. AAAI
- b. A Stake in the Outcome
- c. A4e
- d. International Organization for Standardization

Chapter 7. QUALITY-MANAGEMENT BEST PRACTICES

36. _____ is a class of problem solving methods aimed at identifying the root causes of problems or events. The practice of _____ is predicated on the belief that problems are best solved by attempting to correct or eliminate root causes, as opposed to merely addressing the immediately obvious symptoms. By directing corrective measures at root causes, it is hoped that the likelihood of problem recurrence will be minimized.
   a. 28-hour day
   b. Zero defects
   c. Root cause analysis
   d. 1990 Clean Air Act

37. _____ is a form of communication that typically attempts to persuade potential customers to purchase or to consume more of a particular brand of product or service. 'While now central to the contemporary global economy and the reproduction of global production networks, it is only quite recently that _____ has been more than a marginal influence on patterns of sales and production. The formation of modern _____ was intimately bound up with the emergence of new forms of monopoly capitalism around the end of the 19th and beginning of the 20th century as one element in corporate strategies to create, organize and where possible control markets, especially for mass produced consumer goods.
   a. A4e
   b. Advertising
   c. AAAI
   d. A Stake in the Outcome

38. _____ is a 'method to transform user demands into design quality, to deploy the functions forming quality, and to deploy methods for achieving the design quality into subsystems and component parts, and ultimately to specific elements of the manufacturing process.' , as described by Dr. Yoji Akao, who originally developed _____ in Japan in 1966, when the author combined his work in quality assurance and quality control points with function deployment used in Value Engineering.

_____ is designed to help planners focus on characteristics of a new or existing product or service from the viewpoints of market segments, company, or technology-development needs. The technique yields graphs and matrices.

   a. Learning organization
   b. Hoshin Kanri
   c. 1990 Clean Air Act
   d. Quality function deployment

39. A _____ is a decision support tool that uses a tree-like graph or model of decisions and their possible consequences, including chance event outcomes, resource costs, and utility. _____s are commonly used in operations research, specifically in decision analysis, to help identify a strategy most likely to reach a goal. Another use of _____s is as a descriptive means for calculating conditional probabilities.
   a. 33 Strategies of War
   b. 1990 Clean Air Act
   c. 28-hour day
   d. Decision tree

40. A _____ is a graph (flow chart) depicting the sequence in which a project's terminal elements are to be completed by showing terminal elements and their dependencies.

The work breakdown structure or the product breakdown structure show the 'part-whole' relations. In contrast, the _____ shows the 'before-after' relations.

   a. 1990 Clean Air Act
   b. 33 Strategies of War
   c. 28-hour day
   d. Project network

Chapter 7. QUALITY-MANAGEMENT BEST PRACTICES

41. The _____, is a mathematically based algorithm for scheduling a set of project activities. It is an important tool for effective project management.

It was developed in the 1950s by the Dupont Corporation at about the same time that General Dynamics and the US Navy were developing the Program Evaluation and Review Technique (PERT) Today, it is commonly used with all forms of projects, including construction, software development, research projects, product development, engineering, and plant maintenance, among others.

a. 28-hour day
b. 33 Strategies of War
c. Critical path method
d. 1990 Clean Air Act

42. The _____ is a decision making method for use among groups of many sizes, who want to make their decision quickly, as by a vote, but want everyone's opinions taken into account (as opposed to traditional voting, where only the largest group is considered) . The method of tallying is the difference. First, every member of the group gives their view of the solution, with a short explanation.

a. Nominal group technique
b. Decision model
c. Belief decision matrix
d. Hierarchical Decision Process

43. The Program (or Project) Evaluation and Review Technique, commonly abbreviated _____, is a model for project management designed to analyze and represent the tasks involved in completing a given project.

_____ is a method to analyze the involved tasks in completing a given project, specially the time needed to complete each task, and identifying the minimum time needed to complete the total project.

_____ was developed primarily to simplify the planning and scheduling of large and complex projects.

a. 1990 Clean Air Act
b. 33 Strategies of War
c. 28-hour day
d. PERT

44. In decision theory and estimation theory, the _____ of an estimator, $\hat{\theta}$, of an unknown parameter of the distribution, θ, is the expected value of the loss function

$$R(\theta, \hat{\theta}) = \mathbb{E}_\theta L(\theta, \hat{\theta}) = \int L(\theta, \hat{\theta})\, dP_\theta.$$

where dP_θ is a probability measure parametrized by θ.

- For a scalar parameter θ and a quadratic loss function,

$$L(\theta, \hat{\theta}) = (\theta - \hat{\theta})^2$$

the _____ function becomes the mean squared error of the estimate,

$$R(\theta, \hat{\theta}) = E_\theta (\theta - \hat{\theta})^2$$

- In density estimation, the unknown parameter is probability density itself. The loss function is typically chosen to be a norm in an appropriate function space. For example, for L^2 norm,

$$L(f, \hat{f}) = \|f - \hat{f}\|_2^2$$

the _____ function becomes the mean integrated squared error

$$R(f, \hat{f}) = E\|f - \hat{f}\|^2$$

    a. Linear model
    c. Financial modeling
    b. Risk aversion
    d. Risk

45. _____ is the identification, assessment, and prioritization of risks followed by coordinated and economical application of resources to minimize, monitor, and control the probability and/or impact of unfortunate events.. Risks can come from uncertainty in financial markets, project failures, legal liabilities, credit risk, accidents, natural causes and disasters as well as deliberate attacks from an adversary. Several _____ standards have been developed including the Project Management Institute, the National Institute of Science and Technology, actuarial societies, and ISO standards.
    a. Succession planning
    c. Trademark
    b. Kanban
    d. Risk management

46. In a publicly-held company, an _____ is an operating committee of the Board of Directors, typically charged with oversight of financial reporting and disclosure. Committee members are drawn from members of the Company's board of directors, with a Chairperson selected from among the members. An _____ of a publicly-traded company in the United States is composed of independent and outside directors referred to as non-executive directors, at least one of which is typically a financial expert.
    a. Internal control
    c. A Stake in the Outcome
    b. Internal auditing
    d. Audit committee

47. _____ is a broad label that refers to any individuals or households that use goods and services generated within the economy. The concept of a _____ is used in different contexts, so that the usage and significance of the term may vary.

Chapter 7. QUALITY-MANAGEMENT BEST PRACTICES

Typically when business people and economists talk of _____s they are talking about person as _____, an aggregated commodity item with little individuality other than that expressed in the buy/not-buy decision.

a. 33 Strategies of War
c. 1990 Clean Air Act
b. 28-hour day
d. Consumer

48. The _____ was enacted in 1972 by the United States Congress. It established the United States Consumer Product Safety Commission as an independent agency of the United States federal government and defined its basic authority. The act gives CPSC the power to develop safety standards and pursue recalls for products that present unreasonable or substantial risks of injury or death to consumers.

a. 33 Strategies of War
c. 28-hour day
b. 1990 Clean Air Act
d. Consumer Product Safety Act

49. Quality management can be considered to have three main components: quality control, quality assurance and _____. Quality management is focused not only on product quality, but also the means to achieve it. Quality management therefore uses quality assurance and control of processes as well as products to achieve more consistent quality.

a. Quality Improvement
c. Quality management
b. 28-hour day
d. 1990 Clean Air Act

50. _____ is a separate and emerging business-process management methodology related to traditional Six Sigma. While the tools and order used in Six Sigma require a process to be in place and functioning, _____ has the objective of determining the needs of customers and the business, and driving those needs into the product solution so created. _____ is relevant to the complex system/product synthesis phase, especially in the context of unprecedented system development.

a. 1990 Clean Air Act
c. Design methods
b. 28-hour day
d. Design for Six Sigma

51. _____ is a term used in business and Information Technology (through ITIL) to describe the process of capturing a customer's requirements. Specifically, the _____ is a market research technique that produces a detailed set of customer wants and needs, organized into a hierarchical structure, and then prioritized in terms of relative importance and satisfaction with current alternatives. _____ studies typically consist of both qualitative and quantitative research steps.

a. Business philosophy
c. Voice of the customer
b. Board of governors
d. Goal setting

52. _____ is the term used to refer to the standard framework of guidelines for financial accounting used in any given jurisdiction. _____ includes the standards, conventions, and rules accountants follow in recording and summarizing transactions, and in the preparation of financial statements.

Financial accounting is information that must be assembled and reported objectively.

a. Net income
c. Treasury stock
b. Depreciation
d. Generally accepted accounting principles

Chapter 7. QUALITY-MANAGEMENT BEST PRACTICES

53. _____ is a graphic tool for defining the relationship between customer desires and the firm/product capabilities. It is a part of the Quality Function Deployment (QFD) and it utilizes a planning matrix to relate what the customer wants to how a firm (that produce the products) is going to meet those wants. It looks like a House with correlation matrix as its roof, customer wants versus product features as the main part, competitor evaluation as the porch etc.

   a. Consensus-seeking decision-making
   b. House of quality
   c. Decision Matrix
   d. Health management system

54. _____ are statistical methods developed by Genichi Taguchi to improve the quality of manufactured goods, and more recently also applied to biotechnology, marketing and advertising. Professional statisticians have welcomed the goals and improvements brought about by _____, particularly by Taguchi's development of designs for studying variation, but have criticized the inefficiency of some of Taguchi's proposals.

Taguchi's work includes three principal contributions to statistics:

1. Taguchi loss function;
2. The philosophy of off-line quality control; and
3. Innovations in the design of experiments.

Traditionally, statistical methods have relied on mean-unbiased estimators of treatment effects: Under the conditions of the Gauss-Markov theorem, least squares estimators have minimum variance among all mean-unbiased estimators. The emphasis on comparisons of means also draws (limiting) comfort from the law of large numbers, according to which the sample means converge to the true mean.

   a. 28-hour day
   b. Taguchi methods
   c. Design of experiments
   d. 1990 Clean Air Act

Chapter 8. PROCESS-MANAGEMENT BEST PRACTICES

1. A _____ or business method is a collection of related, structured activities or tasks that produce a specific service or product (serve a particular goal) for a particular customer or customers. It often can be visualized with a flowchart as a sequence of activities.

There are three types of _____es:

1. Management processes, the processes that govern the operation of a system. Typical management processes include 'Corporate Governance' and 'Strategic Management'.
2. Operational processes, processes that constitute the core business and create the primary value stream. Typical operational processes are Purchasing, Manufacturing, Marketing, and Sales.
3. Supporting processes, which support the core processes. Examples include Accounting, Recruitment, Technical support.

A _____ begins with a customer's need and ends with a customer's need fulfillment. Process oriented organizations break down the barriers of structural departments and try to avoid functional silos.

   a. 28-hour day
   b. 1990 Clean Air Act
   c. 33 Strategies of War
   d. Business process

2. _____ is, in computer science and management, an approach aiming at improvements by means of elevating efficiency and effectiveness of the business process that exist within and across organizations. The key to _____ is for organizations to look at their business processes from a 'clean slate' perspective and determine how they can best construct these processes to improve how they conduct business. _____ Cycle.

_____ is also known as _____, Business Process Redesign, Business Transformation, or Business Process Change Management.

   a. Product life cycle
   b. Horizontal integration
   c. Business process reengineering
   d. Personal management interview

3. _____ is the process of comparing the cost, cycle time, productivity, or quality of a specific process or method to another that is widely considered to be an industry standard or best practice. Essentially, _____ provides a snapshot of the performance of your business and helps you understand where you are in relation to a particular standard. The result is often a business case for making changes in order to make improvements.
   a. Cost leadership
   b. Competitive heterogeneity
   c. Complementors
   d. Benchmarking

4. _____ is a systematic approach to help any organization optimize its underlying processes to achieve more efficient results.

The organization may be a for-profit business, a non-profit organization, a government agency, or any other ongoing concern. Most _____ techniques were developed and refined in the manufacturing era, though many of the methodologies (like Six Sigma) have been successfully adapted to work in the predominantly service-based economy of today.

Chapter 8. PROCESS-MANAGEMENT BEST PRACTICES

a. Fix it twice
c. Micromanagement
b. Contingency theory
d. Business process improvement

5. The _____, is a mathematically based algorithm for scheduling a set of project activities. It is an important tool for effective project management.

It was developed in the 1950s by the Dupont Corporation at about the same time that General Dynamics and the US Navy were developing the Program Evaluation and Review Technique (PERT) Today, it is commonly used with all forms of projects, including construction, software development, research projects, product development, engineering, and plant maintenance, among others.

a. 1990 Clean Air Act
c. 33 Strategies of War
b. Critical path method
d. 28-hour day

6. _____ is an inventory strategy that strives to improve the return on investment of a business by reducing in-process inventory and its associated carrying costs. To meet _____ objectives, the process relies on signals between different points in the process. This means the process is often driven by a series of signals, or Kanban , which tell production when to make the next part. Kanban are usually 'tickets' but can be simple visual signals, such as the presence or absence of a part on a shelf. Implemented correctly, _____ can dramatically improve a manufacturing organization's return on investment, quality, and efficiency.

a. 1990 Clean Air Act
c. 33 Strategies of War
b. 28-hour day
d. Just-in-time

7. _____ is a business management strategy, initially implemented by Motorola, that today enjoys widespread application in many sectors of industry.

_____ seeks to improve the quality of process outputs by identifying and removing the causes of defects (errors) and variation in manufacturing and business processes. It uses a set of quality management methods, including statistical methods, and creates a special infrastructure of people within the organization ('Black Belts' etc.)

a. Production line
c. Theory of constraints
b. Takt time
d. Six Sigma

8. _____ is an effective method of monitoring a process through the use of control charts. Control charts enable the use of objective criteria for distinguishing background variation from events of significance based on statistical techniques. Much of its power lies in the ability to monitor both process center and its variation about that center.

a. Statistical process control
c. Process capability
b. Quality control
d. Single Minute Exchange of Die

9. _____ is one of the managerial functions like planning, organizing, staffing and directing. It is an important function because it helps to check the errors and to take the corrective action so that deviation from standards are minimized and stated goals of the organization are achieved in desired manner.According to modern concepts, _____ is a foreseeing action whereas earlier concept of _____ was used only when errors were detected. _____ in management means setting standards, measuring actual performance and taking corrective action.

Chapter 8. PROCESS-MANAGEMENT BEST PRACTICES

a. Control
b. Schedule of reinforcement
c. Turnover
d. Decision tree pruning

10. In organizational development (OD), _____ is a series of actions taken by a Process Owner to identify, analyze and improve existing processes within an organization to meet new goals and objectives. These actions often follow a specific methodology or strategy to create successful results. A sampling of these are listed below.

a. Product innovation
b. Process improvement
c. Letter of resignation
d. Supervisory board

11. _____ is a term that refers both to:

- a formal discipline used to help appraise, or assess, the case for a project or proposal, which itself is a process known as project appraisal; and
- an informal approach to making decisions of any kind.

Under both definitions the process involves, whether explicitly or implicitly, weighing the total expected costs against the total expected benefits of one or more actions in order to choose the best or most profitable option. The formal process is often referred to as either CBA (_____) or BCost-benefit analysis

A hallmark of CBA is that all benefits and all costs are expressed in money terms, and are adjusted for the time value of money, so that all flows of benefits and flows of project costs over time (which tend to occur at different points in time) are expressed on a common basis in terms of their 'present value.' Closely related, but slightly different, formal techniques include Cost-effectiveness analysis, Economic impact analysis, Fiscal impact analysis and Social Return on Investment(SROI) analysis. The latter builds upon the logic of _____, but differs in that it is explicitly designed to inform the practical decision-making of enterprise managers and investors focused on optimising their social and environmental impacts.

a. Kepner-Tregoe
b. Cost-benefit analysis
c. Decision engineering
d. Gittins index

12. _____ refers to the movement of cash into or out of a business or financial product. It is usually measured during a specified, finite period of time. Measurement of _____ can be used

- to determine a project's rate of return or value. The time of _____s into and out of projects are used as inputs in financial models such as internal rate of return, and net present value.
- to determine problems with a business's liquidity. Being profitable does not necessarily mean being liquid. A company can fail because of a shortage of cash, even while profitable.
- as an alternate measure of a business's profits when it is believed that accrual accounting concepts do not represent economic realities. For example, a company may be notionally profitable but generating little operational cash (as may be the case for a company that barters its products rather than selling for cash.) In such a case, the company may be deriving additional operating cash by issuing shares evaluating default risk, re-investment requirements, etc.

_____ is a generic term used differently depending on the context. It may be defined by users for their own purposes.

Chapter 8. PROCESS-MANAGEMENT BEST PRACTICES

a. Cash flow
c. Gross profit

b. Sweat equity
d. Gross profit margin

13. _____ is the discipline of planning, organizing and managing resources to bring about the successful completion of specific project goals and objectives. It is often closely related to and sometimes conflated with Program management.

A project is a finite endeavor--having specific start and completion dates--undertaken to meet particular goals and objectives, usually to bring about beneficial change or added value.

a. Work package
c. Project engineer

b. Precedence diagram
d. Project management

14. _____ is the process of discovering the technological principles of a device, object or system through analysis of its structure, function and operation. It often involves taking something (e.g., a mechanical device, electronic component, or software program) apart and analyzing its workings in detail to be used in maintenance, or to try to make a new device or program that does the same thing without copying anything from the original.

_____ has its origins in the analysis of hardware for commercial or military advantage .

a. 28-hour day
c. Predictive maintenance

b. Reverse engineering
d. 1990 Clean Air Act

15. _____ is a structured approach to transitioning individuals, teams, and organizations from a current state to a desired future state. The current definition of _____ includes both organizational _____ processes and individual _____ models, which together are used to manage the people side of change.

A number of models are available for understanding the transitioning of individuals through the phases of _____ and strengthening organizational development initiative in both government and corporate sectors.

a. 28-hour day
c. 33 Strategies of War

b. 1990 Clean Air Act
d. Change management

16. _____ is a business management strategy aimed at embedding awareness of quality in all organizational processes. _____ has been widely used in manufacturing, education, hospitals, call centers, government, and service industries, as well as NASA space and science programs.

As defined by the International Organization for Standardization (ISO):

'_____ is a management approach for an organization, centered on quality, based on the participation of all its members and aiming at long-term success through customer satisfaction, and benefits to all members of the organization and to society.' ISO 8402:1994

One major aim is to reduce variation from every process so that greater consistency of effort is obtained. (Royse, D., Thyer, B., Padgett D., ' Logan T., 2006)

Chapter 8. PROCESS-MANAGEMENT BEST PRACTICES

a. 28-hour day
b. 1990 Clean Air Act
c. Quality management
d. Total quality management

17. _____ can be considered to have three main components: quality control, quality assurance and quality improvement. _____ is focused not only on product quality, but also the means to achieve it. _____ therefore uses quality assurance and control of processes as well as products to achieve more consistent quality.

a. 28-hour day
b. 1990 Clean Air Act
c. Total quality management
d. Quality management

18. _____ is a class of problem solving methods aimed at identifying the root causes of problems or events. The practice of _____ is predicated on the belief that problems are best solved by attempting to correct or eliminate root causes, as opposed to merely addressing the immediately obvious symptoms. By directing corrective measures at root causes, it is hoped that the likelihood of problem recurrence will be minimized.

a. Zero defects
b. 28-hour day
c. 1990 Clean Air Act
d. Root cause analysis

19.

_____ is a systematic method to improve the 'value' of goods or products and services by using an examination of function. Value, as defined, is the ratio of function to cost. Value can therefore be increased by either improving the function or reducing the cost.

a. Value engineering
b. Cellular manufacturing
c. Capacity planning
d. Master production schedule

20. In corporate finance, _____ or _____ is an estimate of true economic profit after making corrective adjustments to GAAP accounting, including deducting the opportunity cost of equity capital. _____ can be measured as Net Operating Profit After Taxes(or NOPAT) less the money cost of capital. _____ is similar in nature to that of calculating another financial performance measure - Residual Income , however, there are a few complexities involved with coming up with the elements for calculating _____ over RI such as the myriad adjustments that might be made to NOPAT before it is suitable for the formula below.

a. AAAI
b. A4e
c. A Stake in the Outcome
d. Economic value added

21. A _____ is a common type of chart, that represents an algorithm or process, showing the steps as boxes of various kinds, and their order by connecting these with arrows. _____s are used in analyzing, designing, documenting or managing a process or program in various fields.

The first structured method for documenting process flow, the 'flow process chart', was introduced by Frank Gilbreth to members of ASME in 1921 as the presentation 'Process Charts--First Steps in Finding the One Best Way'.

a. 28-hour day
b. 33 Strategies of War
c. 1990 Clean Air Act
d. Flowchart

Chapter 8. PROCESS-MANAGEMENT BEST PRACTICES

22. The _____, widely known as ISO , is an international-standard-setting body composed of representatives from various national standards organizations. Founded on 23 February 1947, the organization promulgates worldwide proprietary industrial and commercial standards. It is headquartered in Geneva, Switzerland.
   a. AAAI
   b. A4e
   c. International Organization for Standardization
   d. A Stake in the Outcome

23. A _____ is a decision support tool that uses a tree-like graph or model of decisions and their possible consequences, including chance event outcomes, resource costs, and utility. _____s are commonly used in operations research, specifically in decision analysis, to help identify a strategy most likely to reach a goal. Another use of _____s is as a descriptive means for calculating conditional probabilities.
   a. 33 Strategies of War
   b. 28-hour day
   c. Decision tree
   d. 1990 Clean Air Act

24. _____ refers to the difference between the cost of materials purchased by a company plus the cost of the labor to assemble a product and the price at which the company sells the product. An example is the price of gasoline at the pump over the price of the oil in it. In national accounts used in macroeconomics, it refers to the contribution of the factors of production, i.e., land, labor, and capital goods, to raising the value of a product and corresponds to the incomes received by the owners of these factors.
   a. Deregulation
   b. Value added
   c. Minimum wage
   d. Rehn-Meidner Model

25. The _____ in statistical process control is a tool used to determine whether a manufacturing or business process is in a state of statistical control or not.

If the chart indicates that the process is currently under control then it can be used with confidence to predict the future performance of the process. If the chart indicates that the process being monitored is not in control, the pattern it reveals can help determine the source of variation to be eliminated to bring the process back into control.

   a. Control chart
   b. Simple moving average
   c. Time series analysis
   d. Failure rate

26. In statistics, a _____ is a graphical display of tabulated frequencies, shown as bars. It shows what proportion of cases fall into each of several categories: it is a form of data binning. The categories are usually specified as non-overlapping intervals of some variable.
   a. Standard deviation
   b. Histogram
   c. Statistics
   d. Correlation

27. A _____, also known as a run-sequence plot is a graph that displays observed data in a time sequence. Often, the data displayed represent some aspect of the output or performance of a manufacturing or other business process.

Run sequence plots are an easy way to graphically summarize a univariate data set.

   a. 1990 Clean Air Act
   b. 33 Strategies of War
   c. 28-hour day
   d. Run chart

Chapter 8. PROCESS-MANAGEMENT BEST PRACTICES

28. A scatter plot is a type of display using Cartesian coordinates to display values for two variables for a set of data.

The data is displayed as a collection of points, each having the value of one variable determining the position on the horizontal axis and the value of the other variable determining the position on the vertical axis. A scatter plot is also called a scatter chart, _____ and scatter graph.

 a. 1990 Clean Air Act
 b. 28-hour day
 c. 33 Strategies of War
 d. Scatter diagram

29. _____ is a separate and emerging business-process management methodology related to traditional Six Sigma. While the tools and order used in Six Sigma require a process to be in place and functioning, _____ has the objective of determining the needs of customers and the business, and driving those needs into the product solution so created. _____ is relevant to the complex system/product synthesis phase, especially in the context of unprecedented system development.
 a. Design methods
 b. 28-hour day
 c. 1990 Clean Air Act
 d. Design for Six Sigma

30. _____ is the term used to refer to the standard framework of guidelines for financial accounting used in any given jurisdiction. _____ includes the standards, conventions, and rules accountants follow in recording and summarizing transactions, and in the preparation of financial statements.

Financial accounting is information that must be assembled and reported objectively.

 a. Depreciation
 b. Treasury stock
 c. Net income
 d. Generally accepted accounting principles

31. _____ is a graphic tool for defining the relationship between customer desires and the firm/product capabilities. It is a part of the Quality Function Deployment (QFD) and it utilizes a planning matrix to relate what the customer wants to how a firm (that produce the products) is going to meet those wants. It looks like a House with correlation matrix as its roof, customer wants versus product features as the main part, competitor evaluation as the porch etc.
 a. Consensus-seeking decision-making
 b. Decision Matrix
 c. House of quality
 d. Health management system

32. _____ is a 'method to transform user demands into design quality, to deploy the functions forming quality, and to deploy methods for achieving the design quality into subsystems and component parts, and ultimately to specific elements of the manufacturing process.' , as described by Dr. Yoji Akao, who originally developed _____ in Japan in 1966, when the author combined his work in quality assurance and quality control points with function deployment used in Value Engineering.

_____ is designed to help planners focus on characteristics of a new or existing product or service from the viewpoints of market segments, company, or technology-development needs. The technique yields graphs and matrices.

 a. Learning organization
 b. Quality function deployment
 c. 1990 Clean Air Act
 d. Hoshin Kanri

Chapter 8. PROCESS-MANAGEMENT BEST PRACTICES

33. _____ is an overall management philosophy introduced by Dr. Eliyahu M. Goldratt in his 1984 book titled The Goal, that is geared to help organizations continually achieve their goal. The title comes from the contention that any manageable system is limited in achieving more of its goal by a very small number of constraints, and that there is always at least one constraint. The _____ process seeks to identify the constraint and restructure the rest of the organization around it, through the use of the Five Focusing Steps.
 a. Six Sigma
 b. Takt time
 c. Production line
 d. Theory of constraints

34. _____ is a term used in business and Information Technology (through ITIL) to describe the process of capturing a customer's requirements. Specifically, the _____ is a market research technique that produces a detailed set of customer wants and needs, organized into a hierarchical structure, and then prioritized in terms of relative importance and satisfaction with current alternatives. _____ studies typically consist of both qualitative and quantitative research steps.
 a. Business philosophy
 b. Board of governors
 c. Voice of the customer
 d. Goal setting

Chapter 9. HUMAN-RESOURCES MANAGEMENT BEST PRACTICES

1. _____ is an increasingly broadening term with which an organization, or other human system describes the combination of traditionally administrative personnel functions with acquisition and application of skills, knowledge and experience, Employee Relations and resource planning at various levels. The field draws upon concepts developed in Industrial/Organizational Psychology and System Theory. _____ has at least two related interpretations depending on context. The original usage derives from political economy and economics, where it was traditionally called labor, one of four factors of production although this perspective is changing as a function of new and ongoing research into more strategic approaches at national levels. This first usage is used more in terms of '_____ development', and can go beyond just organizations to the level of nations. The more traditional usage within corporations and businesses refers to the individuals within a firm or agency, and to the portion of the organization that deals with hiring, firing, training, and other personnel issues, typically referred to as `_____ management'.

   a. Human resource management
   b. Progressive discipline
   c. Bradford Factor
   d. Human resources

2. A _____ is the belief that there is a technique, method, process, activity, incentive or reward that is more effective at delivering a particular outcome than any other technique, method, process, etc. The idea is that with proper processes, checks, and testing, a desired outcome can be delivered with fewer problems and unforeseen complications. _____s can also be defined as the most efficient (least amount of effort) and effective (best results) way of accomplishing a task, based on repeatable procedures that have proven themselves over time for large numbers of people.

   a. Design management
   b. Fix it twice
   c. Hierarchical organization
   d. Best practice

3. The _____ captures an expanded spectrum of values and criteria for measuring organizational success: economic, ecological and social. With the ratification of the United Nations and ICLEI _____ standard for urban and community accounting in early 2007, this became the dominant approach to public sector full cost accounting. Similar UN standards apply to natural capital and human capital measurement to assist in measurements required by _____, e.g. the ecoBudget standard for reporting ecological footprint.

   a. 28-hour day
   b. Triple bottom line
   c. 1990 Clean Air Act
   d. 33 Strategies of War

4. In probability theory, a probability distribution is called _____ if its cumulative distribution function is _____. This is equivalent to saying that for random variables X with the distribution in question, Pr[X = a] = 0 for all real numbers a, i.e.: the probability that X attains the value a is zero, for any number a. If the distribution of X is _____ then X is called a _____ random variable.

   a. Pay Band
   b. Connectionist expert systems
   c. Decision tree pruning
   d. Continuous

5. _____ is a management process whereby delivery (customer valued) processes are constantly evaluated and improved in the light of their efficiency, effectiveness and flexibility.

Some see it as a meta process for most management systems (Business Process Management, Quality Management, Project Management). Deming saw it as part of the 'system' whereby feedback from the process and customer were evaluated against organisational goals.

   a. Sole proprietorship
   b. Critical Success Factor
   c. Continuous Improvement Process
   d. First-mover advantage

Chapter 9. HUMAN-RESOURCES MANAGEMENT BEST PRACTICES

6. _____ is the process of comparing the cost, cycle time, productivity, or quality of a specific process or method to another that is widely considered to be an industry standard or best practice. Essentially, _____ provides a snapshot of the performance of your business and helps you understand where you are in relation to a particular standard. The result is often a business case for making changes in order to make improvements.

   a. Competitive heterogeneity
   b. Complementors
   c. Cost leadership
   d. Benchmarking

7. _____ can be considered to have three main components: quality control, quality assurance and quality improvement. _____ is focused not only on product quality, but also the means to achieve it. _____ therefore uses quality assurance and control of processes as well as products to achieve more consistent quality.

   a. Total quality management
   b. 28-hour day
   c. 1990 Clean Air Act
   d. Quality management

8. _____ is a term used in business and Information Technology (through ITIL) to describe the process of capturing a customer's requirements. Specifically, the _____ is a market research technique that produces a detailed set of customer wants and needs, organized into a hierarchical structure, and then prioritized in terms of relative importance and satisfaction with current alternatives. _____ studies typically consist of both qualitative and quantitative research steps.

   a. Business philosophy
   b. Voice of the customer
   c. Board of governors
   d. Goal setting

9. The general definition of an _____ is an evaluation of a person, organization, system, process, project or product. _____s are performed to ascertain the validity and reliability of information; also to provide an assessment of a system's internal control. The goal of an _____ is to express an opinion on the person / organization/system (etc) in question, under evaluation based on work done on a test basis.

   a. Audit committee
   b. Internal control
   c. A Stake in the Outcome
   d. Audit

10. A _____ is a volunteer group composed of workers (or even students), usually under the leadership of their supervisor (but they can elect a team leader), who are trained to identify, analyse and solve work-related problems and present their solutions to management in order to improve the performance of the organization, and motivate and enrich the work of employees. When matured, true _____s become self-managing, having gained the confidence of management. _____s are an alternative to the dehumanising concept of the Division of Labour, where workers or individuals are treated like robots.

   a. Competency-based job descriptions
   b. Certified in Production and Inventory Management
   c. Connectionist expert systems
   d. Quality circle

11. _____ is an organization's process of defining its strategy and making decisions on allocating its resources to pursue this strategy, including its capital and people. Various business analysis techniques can be used in _____, including SWOT analysis (Strengths, Weaknesses, Opportunities, and Threats) and PEST analysis (Political, Economic, Social, and Technological analysis) or STEER analysis involving Socio-cultural, Technological, Economic, Ecological, and Regulatory factors and EPISTEL (Environment, Political, Informatic, Social, Technological, Economic and Legal)

Chapter 9. HUMAN-RESOURCES MANAGEMENT BEST PRACTICES 93

_____ is the formal consideration of an organization's future course. All _____ deals with at least one of three key questions:

1. 'What do we do?'
2. 'For whom do we do it?'
3. 'How do we excel?'

In business _____, the third question is better phrased 'How can we beat or avoid competition?'. (Bradford and Duncan, page 1.)

a. 1990 Clean Air Act
b. 28-hour day
c. 33 Strategies of War
d. Strategic planning

12. _____ refers to the stock of skills and knowledge embodied in the ability to perform labor so as to produce economic value. It is the skills and knowledge gained by a worker through education and experience. Many early economic theories refer to it simply as labor, one of three factors of production, and consider it to be a fungible resource -- homogeneous and easily interchangeable.

a. Deflation
b. Market structure
c. Human capital
d. Productivity management

13. _____ has been described as the 'process of social influence in which one person can enlist the aid and support of others in the accomplishment of a common task'. A definition more inclusive of followers comes from Alan Keith of Genentech who said '_____ is ultimately about creating a way for people to contribute to making something extraordinary happen.'

_____ is one of the most salient aspects of the organizational context. However, defining _____ has been challenging.

a. Situational leadership
b. 28-hour day
c. Leadership
d. 1990 Clean Air Act

14. _____ is an inventory strategy that strives to improve the return on investment of a business by reducing in-process inventory and its associated carrying costs. To meet _____ objectives, the process relies on signals between different points in the process. This means the process is often driven by a series of signals, or Kanban, which tell production when to make the next part. Kanban are usually 'tickets' but can be simple visual signals, such as the presence or absence of a part on a shelf. Implemented correctly, _____ can dramatically improve a manufacturing organization's return on investment, quality, and efficiency.

a. 1990 Clean Air Act
b. 33 Strategies of War
c. Just-in-time
d. 28-hour day

15. _____ is, in very basic words, a position a firm occupies against its competitors.

According to Michael Porter, the three methods for creating a sustainable _____ are through:

1. Cost leadership

94   *Chapter 9. HUMAN-RESOURCES MANAGEMENT BEST PRACTICES*

2. Differentiation

3. Focus (economics)

    a. Competitive advantage   b. Theory Z
    c. 1990 Clean Air Act   d. 28-hour day

16. _____ is a group creativity technique designed to generate a large number of ideas for the solution of a problem. The method was first popularized in the late 1930s by Alex Faickney Osborn in a book called Applied Imagination. Osborn proposed that groups could double their creative output with _____.

    a. Adam Smith   b. Brainstorming
    c. Affiliation   d. Abraham Harold Maslow

17. In decision theory and estimation theory, the _____ of an estimator, $\hat{\theta}$, of an unknown parameter of the distribution, θ, is the expected value of the loss function

$$R(\theta, \hat{\theta}) = \mathbb{E}_\theta L(\theta, \hat{\theta}) = \int L(\theta, \hat{\theta})\, dP_\theta.$$

where dP_θ is a probability measure parametrized by θ.

- For a scalar parameter θ and a quadratic loss function,

$$L(\theta, \hat{\theta}) = (\theta - \hat{\theta})^2$$

    the _____ function becomes the mean squared error of the estimate,

$$R(\theta, \hat{\theta}) = E_\theta (\theta - \hat{\theta})^2$$

- In density estimation, the unknown parameter is probability density itself. The loss function is typically chosen to be a norm in an appropriate function space. For example, for L^2 norm,

$$L(f, \hat{f}) = \|f - \hat{f}\|_2^2$$

    the _____ function becomes the mean integrated squared error

$$R(f, \hat{f}) = E\|f - \hat{f}\|^2$$

Chapter 9. HUMAN-RESOURCES MANAGEMENT BEST PRACTICES

a. Linear model
b. Risk
c. Risk aversion
d. Financial modeling

18.

The terms _____ and positive action refer to policies that take race, ethnicity, or gender into consideration in an attempt to promote equal opportunity. The focus of such policies ranges from employment and education to public contracting and health programs. The impetus towards _____ is twofold: to maximize diversity in all levels of society, along with its presumed benefits, and to redress perceived disadvantages due to overt, institutional, or involuntary discrimination.

a. Adam Smith
b. Abraham Harold Maslow
c. Affirmative action
d. Affiliation

19. The _____ of 1990 (ADA) is the short title of United States (Pub.L. 101-336, 104 Stat. 327, enacted July 26, 1990), codified at 42 U.S.C. § 12101 et seq. It was signed into law on July 26, 1990, by President George H. W. Bush, and later amended with changes effective January 1, 2009. The ADA is a wide-ranging civil rights law that prohibits, under certain circumstances, discrimination based on disability. It affords similar protections against discrimination to Americans with disabilities as the Civil Rights Act of 1964,

a. Australian labour law
b. Employment discrimination
c. Americans with Disabilities Act
d. Equal Pay Act of 1963

20. _____ generally refers to a list of all planned expenses and revenues. It is a plan for saving and spending. A _____ is an important concept in microeconomics, which uses a _____ line to illustrate the trade-offs between two or more goods.

a. Budget
b. 1990 Clean Air Act
c. 33 Strategies of War
d. 28-hour day

21. The _____ of 1985 is a law passed by the U.S. Congress and signed by President Reagan that, among other things, mandates an insurance program giving some employees the ability to continue health insurance coverage after leaving employment. _____ includes amendments to the Employee Retirement Income Security Act of 1974 (ERISA.) The law deals with a great variety of subjects, such as tobacco price supports, railroads, private pension plans, disability insurance, and the postal service, but it is perhaps best known for Title X, which amends the Internal Revenue Code to deny income tax deductions to employers for contributions to a group health plan unless such plan meets certain continuing coverage requirements.

a. 1990 Clean Air Act
b. Consolidated Omnibus Budget Reconciliation Act
c. 33 Strategies of War
d. 28-hour day

22. The U.S. _____ of 1988 ('_____') generally prevents employers from using lie detector tests, either for pre-employment screening or during the course of employment, with certain exemptions. Employers generally may not require or request any employee or job applicant to take a lie detector test, or discharge, discipline, or discriminate against an employee or job applicant for refusing to take a test or for exercising other rights under the Act. In addition, employers are required to display a poster in the workplace explaining the _____ for their employees.

a. A Stake in the Outcome
b. AAAI
c. A4e
d. Employee Polygraph Protection Act

23. _____ is an advertisement in which a particular product specifically mentions a competitor by name for the express purpose of showing why the competitor is inferior to the product naming it.

This should not be confused with parody advertisements, where a fictional product is being advertised for the purpose of poking fun at the particular advertisement, nor should it be confused with the use of a coined brand name for the purpose of comparing the product without actually naming an actual competitor. ('Wikipedia tastes better and is less filling than the Encyclopedia Galactica.')

In the 1980s, during what has been referred to as the cola wars, soft-drink manufacturer Pepsi ran a series of advertisements where people, caught on hidden camera, in a blind taste test, chose Pepsi over rival Coca-Cola.

 a. 33 Strategies of War
 b. Comparative advertising
 c. 28-hour day
 d. 1990 Clean Air Act

24. _____ is a concept in ethics with several meanings. It is often used synonymously with such concepts as responsibility, answerability, enforcement, blameworthiness, liability and other terms associated with the expectation of account-giving. As an aspect of governance, it has been central to discussions related to problems in both the public and private (corporation) worlds.

 a. Usury
 b. Accountability
 c. A4e
 d. A Stake in the Outcome

25. _____ is one of the managerial functions like planning, organizing, staffing and directing. It is an important function because it helps to check the errors and to take the corrective action so that deviation from standards are minimized and stated goals of the organization are achieved in desired manner. According to modern concepts, _____ is a foreseeing action whereas earlier concept of _____ was used only when errors were detected. _____ in management means setting standards, measuring actual performance and taking corrective action.

 a. Decision tree pruning
 b. Control
 c. Schedule of reinforcement
 d. Turnover

26. The _____ 1970 is an Act of the United Kingdom Parliament which prohibits any less favourable treatment between men and women in terms of pay and conditions of employment. It came into force on 29 December 1975. The term pay is interpreted in a broad sense to include, on top of wages, things like holidays, pension rights, company perks and some kinds of bonuses.

 a. Equal Pay Act
 b. Oncale v. Sundowner Offshore Services
 c. Australian labour law
 d. Architectural Barriers Act of 1968

27. The _____ of 1938 (_____, ch. 676, 52 Stat. 1060, June 25, 1938, 29 U.S.C. ch.8), also called the Wages and Hours Bill, is United States federal law that applies to employees engaged in interstate commerce or employed by an enterprise engaged in commerce or in the production of goods for commerce, unless the employer can claim an exemption from coverage. The _____ established a national minimum wage, guaranteed time and a half for overtime in certain jobs, and prohibited most employment of minors in 'oppressive child labor,' a term defined in the statute.

 a. Family and Medical Leave Act of 1993
 b. Board of directors
 c. Joint venture
 d. Fair Labor Standards Act

Chapter 9. HUMAN-RESOURCES MANAGEMENT BEST PRACTICES

28. The _____ is a United States labor law allowing an employee to take unpaid leave due to a serious health condition that makes the employee unable to perform his job or to care for a sick family member or to care for a new son or daughter (including by birth, adoption or foster care.) The bill was among the first signed into law by President Bill Clinton in his first term.
   a. Sarbanes-Oxley Act of 2002
   b. Harvester Judgment
   c. Contributory negligence
   d. Family and Medical Leave Act of 1993

29. The _____ of 1977 (15 U.S.C. §§ 78dd-1, et seq.) is a United States federal law known primarily for two of its main provisions, one that addresses accounting transparency requirements under the Securities Exchange Act of 1934 and another concerning bribery of foreign officials.
   a. Social Security Act of 1965
   b. Limited liability
   c. Foreign Corrupt Practices Act
   d. Meritor Savings Bank v. Vinson

30. _____ are conventions, treaties and recommendations designed to eliminate unjust and inhumane labour practices. The primary inernational agency charged with developing such standards is the International Labour Organization (ILO.) Established in 1919, the ILO advocates international standards as essential for the eradication of labour conditions involving 'injustice, hardship and privation'.
   a. Airbus Industrie
   b. Anaconda Copper
   c. Airbus SAS
   d. International labour standards

31. _____ is a cross-disciplinary area concerned with protecting the safety, health and welfare of people engaged in work or employment. The goal of all _____ programs is to foster a work free safe environment. As a secondary effect, it may also protect co-workers, family members, employers, customers, suppliers, nearby communities, and other members of the public who are impacted by the workplace environment.
   a. Occupational Safety and Health
   b. A4e
   c. AAAI
   d. A Stake in the Outcome

32. The _____ is the primary federal law which governs occupational health and safety in the private sector and federal government in the United States. It was enacted by Congress in 1970 and was signed by President Richard Nixon on December 29, 1970. Its main goal is to ensure that employers provide employees with an environment free from recognized hazards, such as exposure to toxic chemicals, excessive noise levels, mechanical dangers, heat or cold stress, or unsanitary conditions.
   a. Unemployment and Farm Relief Act
   b. United States Department of Justice
   c. Unemployment Action Center
   d. Occupational Safety and Health Act

33. _____ is a contract between two parties, one being the employer and the other being the employee. An employee may be defined as: 'A person in the service of another under any contract of hire, express or implied, oral or written, where the employer has the power or right to control and direct the employee in the material details of how the work is to be performed.' Black's Law Dictionary page 471 (5th ed. 1979.)
   a. Employment counsellor
   b. Employment rate
   c. Exit interview
   d. Employment

Chapter 9. HUMAN-RESOURCES MANAGEMENT BEST PRACTICES

34. _____ occurs when expectant women are fired, not hired, or otherwise discriminated against due to their pregnancy or intention to become pregnant. Common forms of _____ include not being hired due to visible pregnancy or likelihood of becoming pregnant, being fired after informing an employer of one's pregnancy, being fired after maternity leave, and receiving a pay dock due to pregnancy. In the United States, since 1978, employers are legally bound to provide what insurance, leave pay, and additional support that would be bestowed upon any employee with medical leave or disability.
   a. 1990 Clean Air Act
   b. 28-hour day
   c. 33 Strategies of War
   d. Pregnancy Discrimination

35. _____ is the point where a person stops employment completely. A person may also semi-retire and keep some sort of _____ job, out of choice rather than necessity. This usually happens upon reaching a determined age, when physical conditions don't allow the person to work any more (by illness or accident), or even for personal choice (usually in the presence of an adequate pension or personal savings.)
   a. Termination of employment
   b. Retirement
   c. Wrongful dismissal
   d. Severance package

36. The _____ requires the Federal government to investigate and pursue trusts, companies and organizations suspected of violating the Act. It was the first United States Federal statute to limit cartels and monopolies, and today still forms the basis for most antitrust litigation by the federal government.
   a. Sherman Antitrust Act
   b. 1990 Clean Air Act
   c. 33 Strategies of War
   d. 28-hour day

37. The _____ of 1994 (USERRA) was signed into law by U.S. President Bill Clinton on October 13, 1994 to protect the civilian employment of non-full time military service members in the United States called to active duty. The law applies to all United States uniformed services and their respective reserve components.

USERRA clarifies and strengthens the Veterans' Reemployment Rights (VRR) Statute by protecting civilian job rights and benefits for veterans, members of reserve components, and even individuals activated by the President of the United States to provide Federal Response for National Emergencies.

   a. Uniformed Services Employment and Reemployment Rights Act
   b. Occupational disease
   c. Intent
   d. Employment protection legislation

38. The _____ is a 1935 United States federal law that limits the means with which employers may react to workers in the private sector that organize labor unions, engage in collective bargaining, and take part in strikes and other forms of concerted activity in support of their demands. The Act does not, on the other hand, cover those workers who are covered by the Railway Labor Act, agricultural employees, domestic employees, supervisors, independent contractors and some close relatives of individual employers.

It was in a context of severe economic troubles that the Wagner Act came into effect.

   a. 1990 Clean Air Act
   b. 28-hour day
   c. 33 Strategies of War
   d. National Labor Relations Act

Chapter 9. HUMAN-RESOURCES MANAGEMENT BEST PRACTICES

39. The field of _____ looks at the relationship between management and workers, particularly groups of workers represented by a union.

_____ is an important factor in analyzing 'varieties of capitalism', such as neocorporatism, social democracy, and neoliberalism

- a. Overtime
- b. Organizational effectiveness
- c. Informal organization
- d. Industrial relations

40. The _____ is a United States labor law that regulates labor unions' internal affairs and their officials' relationships with employers.

Enacted in 1959 after revelations of corruption and undemocratic practices in the International Brotherhood of Teamsters, International Longshoremen's Association, United Mine Workers and other unions received wide public attention, the Act requires unions to hold secret elections for local union offices on a regular basis and provides for review by the United States Department of Labor of union members' claims of improper election activity.

Other provisions of the law:

- Bar members of the Communist Party and convicted felons from holding union office.
- Require unions to submit annual financial reports to the DOL.
- Declare that every union officer must act as a fiduciary in handling the assets and conducting the affairs of the union.
- Limit the power of unions to put subordinate bodies in trusteeship, a temporary suspension of democratic processes within a union.
- Provide certain minimum standards before a union may expel or take other disciplinary action against a member of the union.

The LMRDA covers both workers and unions covered by the National Labor Relations Act and workers and unions in the railroad and airline industries, who are covered by the Railway Labor Act. The LMRDA does not, as a general rule, cover public sector employees, who are not covered by either the NLRA or the RLA.

- a. Civil Rights Act of 1964
- b. Civil Rights Act of 1875
- c. Labor Management Reporting and Disclosure Act
- d. Right-to-work laws

41. The _____ is a United States federal law that governs labor relations in the railway and airline industries. The Act, passed in 1926 and amended in 1936 to apply to the airline industry, seeks to substitute bargaining, arbitration and mediation for strikes as a means of resolving labor disputes.

After the national railroad strike of 1877, which was put down only with the intervention of federal troops, Congress passed the Arbitration Act of 1888, which authorized the creation of arbitration panels with the power to investigate the causes of labor disputes and to issue non-binding arbitration awards.

a. Racketeer Influenced and Corrupt Organizations Act
b. Patent
c. Leave of absence
d. Railway Labor Act

42. _____ is the process of learning a new skill or trade, often in response to a change in the economic environment. Generally it reflects changes in profession choice rather than an 'upward' movement in the same field.

There is some controversy surrounding the use of _____ to offset economic changes caused by free trade and automation.

a. Compliance Training
b. Suspension training
c. Krauthammer
d. Retraining

43. The _____ is the labour pool in employment. It is generally used to describe those working for a single company or industry, but can also apply to a geographic region like a city, country, state, etc. The term generally excludes the employers or management, and implies those involved in manual labour.

a. Division of labour
b. Workforce
c. Pink-collar worker
d. Work-life balance

Chapter 10. ACCOUNTING, TREASURY, AND FINANCE-MANAGEMENT BEST PRACTICES   101

1. _____ generally refers to a list of all planned expenses and revenues. It is a plan for saving and spending. A _____ is an important concept in microeconomics, which uses a _____ line to illustrate the trade-offs between two or more goods.

   a. 33 Strategies of War
   b. 1990 Clean Air Act
   c. 28-hour day
   d. Budget

2. _____ is the planning process used to determine whether a firm's long term investments such as new machinery, replacement machinery, new plants, new products, and research development projects are worth pursuing. It is budget for major capital, or investment, expenditures.

Many formal methods are used in _____, including the techniques such as

- Net present value
- Profitability index
- Internal rate of return
- Modified Internal Rate of Return
- Equivalent annuity

These methods use the incremental cash flows from each potential investment, or project. Techniques based on accounting earnings and accounting rules are sometimes used - though economists consider this to be improper - such as the accounting rate of return, and 'return on investment.' Simplified and hybrid methods are used as well, such as payback period and discounted payback period.

   a. Restricted stock
   b. Gross profit margin
   c. Gross profit
   d. Capital budgeting

3. The _____ of a company or public agency is the corporate officer primarily responsible for managing the financial risks of the business or agency. This officer is also responsible for financial planning and record-keeping, as well as financial reporting to higher management. (In recent years, however, the role has expanded to encompass communicating financial performance and forecasts to the analyst community.)

   a. Chief financial officer
   b. 33 Strategies of War
   c. 1990 Clean Air Act
   d. 28-hour day

4. _____ is, in very basic words, a position a firm occupies against its competitors.

According to Michael Porter, the three methods for creating a sustainable _____ are through:

1. Cost leadership

2. Differentiation

3. Focus (economics)

   a. 1990 Clean Air Act
   b. Theory Z
   c. 28-hour day
   d. Competitive advantage

Chapter 10. ACCOUNTING, TREASURY, AND FINANCE-MANAGEMENT BEST PRACTICES

5. _____ are formal records of the financial activities of a business, person, or other entity. In British English, including United Kingdom company law, _____ are often referred to as accounts, although the term _____ is also used, particularly by accountants.

_____ provide an overview of a business or person's financial condition in both short and long term.

- a. 28-hour day
- b. Financial statements
- c. 33 Strategies of War
- d. 1990 Clean Air Act

6. A _____ is the belief that there is a technique, method, process, activity, incentive or reward that is more effective at delivering a particular outcome than any other technique, method, process, etc. The idea is that with proper processes, checks, and testing, a desired outcome can be delivered with fewer problems and unforeseen complications. _____s can also be defined as the most efficient (least amount of effort) and effective (best results) way of accomplishing a task, based on repeatable procedures that have proven themselves over time for large numbers of people.

- a. Design management
- b. Hierarchical organization
- c. Best practice
- d. Fix it twice

7. In probability theory, a probability distribution is called _____ if its cumulative distribution function is _____. This is equivalent to saying that for random variables X with the distribution in question, Pr[X = a] = 0 for all real numbers a, i.e.: the probability that X attains the value a is zero, for any number a. If the distribution of X is _____ then X is called a _____ random variable.

- a. Pay Band
- b. Connectionist expert systems
- c. Continuous
- d. Decision tree pruning

8. _____ is a management process whereby delivery (customer valued) processes are constantly evaluated and improved in the light of their efficiency, effectiveness and flexibility.

Some see it as a meta process for most management systems (Business Process Management, Quality Management, Project Management). Deming saw it as part of the 'system' whereby feedback from the process and customer were evaluated against organisational goals.

- a. First-mover advantage
- b. Critical Success Factor
- c. Sole proprietorship
- d. Continuous Improvement Process

9. A _____ is a list of the general tasks and responsibilities of a position. Typically, it also includes to whom the position reports, specifications such as the qualifications needed by the person in the job, salary range for the position, etc. A _____ is usually developed by conducting a job analysis, which includes examining the tasks and sequences of tasks necessary to perform the job.

- a. Recruitment advertising
- b. Recruitment
- c. Job description
- d. Recruitment Process Insourcing

10. _____ can be considered to have three main components: quality control, quality assurance and quality improvement. _____ is focused not only on product quality, but also the means to achieve it. _____ therefore uses quality assurance and control of processes as well as products to achieve more consistent quality.

Chapter 10. ACCOUNTING, TREASURY, AND FINANCE-MANAGEMENT BEST PRACTICES

a. Quality management
b. 1990 Clean Air Act
c. 28-hour day
d. Total quality management

11. _____ is a term used in business and Information Technology (through ITIL) to describe the process of capturing a customer's requirements. Specifically, the _____ is a market research technique that produces a detailed set of customer wants and needs, organized into a hierarchical structure, and then prioritized in terms of relative importance and satisfaction with current alternatives. _____ studies typically consist of both qualitative and quantitative research steps.

a. Business philosophy
b. Board of governors
c. Voice of the customer
d. Goal setting

12. The general definition of an _____ is an evaluation of a person, organization, system, process, project or product. _____s are performed to ascertain the validity and reliability of information; also to provide an assessment of a system's internal control. The goal of an _____ is to express an opinion on the person / organization/system (etc) in question, under evaluation based on work done on a test basis.

a. Audit committee
b. A Stake in the Outcome
c. Audit
d. Internal control

13. An _____ is any party that makes an investment.

The term has taken on a specific meaning in finance to describe the particular types of people and companies that regularly purchase equity or debt securities for financial gain in exchange for funding an expanding company. Less frequently, the term is applied to parties who purchase real estate, currency, commodity derivatives, personal property, or other assets.

a. A Stake in the Outcome
b. A4e
c. AAAI
d. Investor

14. A _____ is a volunteer group composed of workers (or even students), usually under the leadership of their supervisor (but they can elect a team leader), who are trained to identify, analyse and solve work-related problems and present their solutions to management in order to improve the performance of the organization, and motivate and enrich the work of employees. When matured, true _____s become self-managing, having gained the confidence of management. _____s are an alternative to the dehumanising concept of the Division of Labour, where workers or individuals are treated like robots.

a. Competency-based job descriptions
b. Connectionist expert systems
c. Certified in Production and Inventory Management
d. Quality circle

15. In business, operating margin, operating income margin, operating profit margin or _____ is the ratio of operating income (operating profit in the UK) divided by net sales, usually presented in percent.

(Relevant figures in italics)

Chapter 10. ACCOUNTING, TREASURY, AND FINANCE-MANAGEMENT BEST PRACTICES

It is a measurement of what proportion of a company's revenue is left over, before taxes and other indirect costs (such as rent, bonus, interest, etc.), after paying for variable costs of production as wages, raw materials, etc. A good operating margin is needed for a company to be able to pay for its fixed costs, such as interest on debt.

- a. Rate of return
- b. P/E ratio
- c. Return on equity
- d. Return on sales

16. A _____ or chief executive is one of the highest-ranking corporate officer (executive) or administrator in charge of total management. An individual selected as President and _____ of a corporation, company, organization, or agency, reports to the board of directors. In internal communication and press releases, many companies capitalize the term and those of other high positions, even when they are not proper nouns.

- a. Chief brand officer
- b. Financial analyst
- c. Purchasing manager
- d. Chief executive officer

17. _____ has been described as the 'process of social influence in which one person can enlist the aid and support of others in the accomplishment of a common task'. A definition more inclusive of followers comes from Alan Keith of Genentech who said '_____ is ultimately about creating a way for people to contribute to making something extraordinary happen.'

_____ is one of the most salient aspects of the organizational context. However, defining _____ has been challenging.

- a. 28-hour day
- b. 1990 Clean Air Act
- c. Situational leadership
- d. Leadership

18. _____ is an organization's process of defining its strategy and making decisions on allocating its resources to pursue this strategy, including its capital and people. Various business analysis techniques can be used in _____, including SWOT analysis (Strengths, Weaknesses, Opportunities, and Threats) and PEST analysis (Political, Economic, Social, and Technological analysis) or STEER analysis involving Socio-cultural, Technological, Economic, Ecological, and Regulatory factors and EPISTEL (Environment, Political, Informatic, Social, Technological, Economic and Legal)

_____ is the formal consideration of an organization's future course. All _____ deals with at least one of three key questions:

1. 'What do we do?'
2. 'For whom do we do it?'
3. 'How do we excel?'

In business _____, the third question is better phrased 'How can we beat or avoid competition?'. (Bradford and Duncan, page 1.)

- a. Strategic planning
- b. 33 Strategies of War
- c. 1990 Clean Air Act
- d. 28-hour day

Chapter 10. ACCOUNTING, TREASURY, AND FINANCE-MANAGEMENT BEST PRACTICES

19. While _____ literally refers to a person responsible for the performance of duties involved in running an organization, the exact meaning of the role is variable, depending on the organization.

While there is no clear line between executive or principal and inferior officers, principal officers are high-level officials in the executive branch of U.S. government such as department heads of independent agencies. In Humphrey's Executor v. United States, 295 U.S. 602 (1935), the Court distinguished between _____s and quasi-legislative or quasi-judicial officers by stating that the former serve at the pleasure of the President and may be removed at his discretion.

   a. Executive officer
   b. Easement
   c. Australian Fair Pay and Conditions Standard
   d. Unreported employment

20. _____ is the process of comparing the cost, cycle time, productivity, or quality of a specific process or method to another that is widely considered to be an industry standard or best practice. Essentially, _____ provides a snapshot of the performance of your business and helps you understand where you are in relation to a particular standard. The result is often a business case for making changes in order to make improvements.

   a. Complementors
   b. Cost leadership
   c. Competitive heterogeneity
   d. Benchmarking

21. _____ is subcontracting a process, such as product design or manufacturing, to a third-party company. The decision to outsource is often made in the interest of lowering cost or making better use of time and energy costs, redirecting or conserving energy directed at the competencies of a particular business, or to make more efficient use of land, labor, capital, (information) technology and resources. _____ became part of the business lexicon during the 1980s.

   a. Operant conditioning
   b. Unemployment insurance
   c. Opinion leadership
   d. Outsourcing

22. A _____ or business method is a collection of related, structured activities or tasks that produce a specific service or product (serve a particular goal) for a particular customer or customers. It often can be visualized with a flowchart as a sequence of activities.

There are three types of _____ es:

1. Management processes, the processes that govern the operation of a system. Typical management processes include 'Corporate Governance' and 'Strategic Management'.
2. Operational processes, processes that constitute the core business and create the primary value stream. Typical operational processes are Purchasing, Manufacturing, Marketing, and Sales.
3. Supporting processes, which support the core processes. Examples include Accounting, Recruitment, Technical support.

A _____ begins with a customer's need and ends with a customer's need fulfillment. Process oriented organizations break down the barriers of structural departments and try to avoid functional silos.

   a. 1990 Clean Air Act
   b. Business process
   c. 28-hour day
   d. 33 Strategies of War

106 Chapter 10. ACCOUNTING, TREASURY, AND FINANCE-MANAGEMENT BEST PRACTICES

23. _____ is, in computer science and management, an approach aiming at improvements by means of elevating efficiency and effectiveness of the business process that exist within and across organizations. The key to _____ is for organizations to look at their business processes from a 'clean slate' perspective and determine how they can best construct these processes to improve how they conduct business. _____ Cycle.

_____ is also known as _____, Business Process Redesign, Business Transformation, or Business Process Change Management.

a. Business process reengineering
b. Product life cycle
c. Horizontal integration
d. Personal management interview

24. _____ is the process by which an organization deals with any major unpredictable event that threatens to harm the organization, its stakeholders, or the general public. Three elements are common to most definitions of crisis: (a) a threat to the organization, (b) the element of surprise, and (c) a short decision time.

Whereas risk management involves assessing potential threats and finding the best ways to avoid those threats, _____ involves dealing with the disasters after they have occurred.

a. Business value
b. Capability management
c. C-A-K-E
d. Crisis management

25. _____ is a term that refers both to:

- a formal discipline used to help appraise, or assess, the case for a project or proposal, which itself is a process known as project appraisal; and
- an informal approach to making decisions of any kind.

Under both definitions the process involves, whether explicitly or implicitly, weighing the total expected costs against the total expected benefits of one or more actions in order to choose the best or most profitable option. The formal process is often referred to as either CBA (_____) or BCost-benefit analysis

A hallmark of CBA is that all benefits and all costs are expressed in money terms, and are adjusted for the time value of money, so that all flows of benefits and flows of project costs over time (which tend to occur at different points in time) are expressed on a common basis in terms of their 'present value.' Closely related, but slightly different, formal techniques include Cost-effectiveness analysis, Economic impact analysis, Fiscal impact analysis and Social Return on Investment(SROI) analysis. The latter builds upon the logic of _____, but differs in that it is explicitly designed to inform the practical decision-making of enterprise managers and investors focused on optimising their social and environmental impacts.

a. Kepner-Tregoe
b. Decision engineering
c. Gittins index
d. Cost-benefit analysis

Chapter 10. ACCOUNTING, TREASURY, AND FINANCE-MANAGEMENT BEST PRACTICES

26. In accounting and auditing, _____ is defined as a process effected by an organization's structure, work and authority flows, people and management information systems, designed to help the organization accomplish specific goals or objectives. It is a means by which an organization's resources are directed, monitored, and measured. It plays an important role in preventing and detecting fraud and protecting the organization's resources, both physical (e.g., machinery and property) and intangible (e.g., reputation or intellectual property such as trademarks.)
   a. A Stake in the Outcome
   b. Internal control
   c. Audit committee
   d. Internal auditing

27. _____ is one of the managerial functions like planning, organizing, staffing and directing. It is an important function because it helps to check the errors and to take the corrective action so that deviation from standards are minimized and stated goals of the organization are achieved in desired manner. According to modern concepts, _____ is a foreseeing action whereas earlier concept of _____ was used only when errors were detected. _____ in management means setting standards, measuring actual performance and taking corrective action.
   a. Schedule of reinforcement
   b. Turnover
   c. Decision tree pruning
   d. Control

28. In decision theory and estimation theory, the _____ of an estimator, $\hat{\theta}$, of an unknown parameter of the distribution, θ, is the expected value of the loss function

$$R(\theta, \hat{\theta}) = \mathbb{E}_\theta L(\theta, \hat{\theta}) = \int L(\theta, \hat{\theta})\, dP_\theta.$$

where dP_θ is a probability measure parametrized by θ.

- For a scalar parameter θ and a quadratic loss function,

$$L(\theta, \hat{\theta}) = (\theta - \hat{\theta})^2$$

  the _____ function becomes the mean squared error of the estimate,

$$R(\theta, \hat{\theta}) = E_\theta(\theta - \hat{\theta})^2$$

- In density estimation, the unknown parameter is probability density itself. The loss function is typically chosen to be a norm in an appropriate function space. For example, for L^2 norm,

$$L(f, \hat{f}) = \|f - \hat{f}\|_2^2$$

  the _____ function becomes the mean integrated squared error

$$R(f, \hat{f}) = E\|f - \hat{f}\|^2$$

a. Linear model
c. Financial modeling
b. Risk aversion
d. Risk

29. _____ is the identification, assessment, and prioritization of risks followed by coordinated and economical application of resources to minimize, monitor, and control the probability and/or impact of unfortunate events.. Risks can come from uncertainty in financial markets, project failures, legal liabilities, credit risk, accidents, natural causes and disasters as well as deliberate attacks from an adversary. Several _____ standards have been developed including the Project Management Institute, the National Institute of Science and Technology, actuarial societies, and ISO standards.

a. Kanban
c. Succession planning
b. Trademark
d. Risk management

30. In a publicly-held company, an _____ is an operating committee of the Board of Directors, typically charged with oversight of financial reporting and disclosure. Committee members are drawn from members of the Company's board of directors, with a Chairperson selected from among the members. An _____ of a publicly-traded company in the United States is composed of independent and outside directors referred to as non-executive directors, at least one of which is typically a financial expert.

a. Internal auditing
c. Audit committee
b. Internal control
d. A Stake in the Outcome

31. _____ is a step in a risk management process. _____ is the determination of quantitative or qualitative value of risk related to a concrete situation and a recognized threat (also called hazard.) Quantitative _____ requires calculations of two components of risk: R, the magnitude of the potential loss L, and the probability p, that the loss will occur.

a. Quality assurance
c. 28-hour day
b. 1990 Clean Air Act
d. Risk assessment

32. The _____ of 2002 (Pub.L. 107-204, 116 Stat. 745, enacted July 30, 2002), also known as the Public Company Accounting Reform and Investor Protection Act of 2002 and commonly called Sarbanes-Oxley, Sarbox or SOX, is a United States federal law enacted on July 30, 2002, as a reaction to a number of major corporate and accounting scandals including those affecting Enron, Tyco International, Adelphia, Peregrine Systems and WorldCom.

a. Fair Labor Standards Act
c. Sarbanes-Oxley Act of 2002
b. Letter of credit
d. Sarbanes-Oxley Act

33. The _____ of 1968 is a United States federal law designed to protect consumers in credit transactions, by requiring clear disclosure of key terms of the lending arrangement and all costs. The statute is contained in Title I of the Consumer Credit Protection Act, as amended (15 U.S.C. § 1601 et seq.).

a. 28-hour day
c. Fair Credit Reporting Act
b. 1990 Clean Air Act
d. Truth in Lending Act

34. The _____ of 1977 (15 U.S.C. §§ 78dd-1, et seq.) is a United States federal law known primarily for two of its main provisions, one that addresses accounting transparency requirements under the Securities Exchange Act of 1934 and another concerning bribery of foreign officials.

a. Social Security Act of 1965
c. Foreign Corrupt Practices Act
b. Meritor Savings Bank v. Vinson
d. Limited liability

Chapter 10. ACCOUNTING, TREASURY, AND FINANCE-MANAGEMENT BEST PRACTICES

35. The _____, also known as the RFPA is a United States Act that gives the customers of financial institutions the right to some level of privacy from government searches. Before the Act was passed, the United States government did not have to tell customers that they were accessing their records, and customers did not have the right to prevent such actions.

   a. Right to Financial Privacy Act
   b. Comprehensive Environmental Response, Compensation, and Liability Act
   c. Corporate governance
   d. National treatment

36. The _____ of 1914, (October 151914, ch. 323, 38 Stat. 730, codified at 15 U.S.C. § 12-27, 29 U.S.C. § 52-53), was enacted in the United States to add further substance to the U.S. antitrust law regime by seeking to prevent anticompetitive practices in their incipiency. That regime started with the Sherman Antitrust Act of 1890, the first Federal law outlawing practices considered harmful to consumers (monopolies and cartels). The Clayton act specified particular prohibited conduct, the three-level enforcement scheme,the exemptions, and the remedial measures.

   a. Legal working age
   b. Munn v. Illinois
   c. Clayton Antitrust Act
   d. Long Service Leave

37. The _____ is a United States federal law that provides for extended criminal penalties and a civil cause of action for acts performed as part of an ongoing criminal organization. RICO was enacted by section 901(a) of the Organized Crime Control Act of 1970 (Pub.L. 91-452, 84 Stat.

   a. Negligence in employment
   b. Racketeer Influenced and Corrupt Organizations Act
   c. Business valuation
   d. Minimum wage law

38. The _____ of 1936 (or Anti-Price Discrimination Act, 15 U.S.C. § 13) is a United States federal law that prohibits what were considered, at the time of passage, to be anticompetitive practices by producers, specifically price discrimination. It grew out of practices in which chain stores were allowed to purchase goods at lower prices than other retailers.

   a. Privity
   b. Labor Management Reporting and Disclosure Act
   c. Robinson-Patman Act
   d. Bona fide occupational qualification

39. The _____ requires the Federal government to investigate and pursue trusts, companies and organizations suspected of violating the Act. It was the first United States Federal statute to limit cartels and monopolies, and today still forms the basis for most antitrust litigation by the federal government.

   a. 28-hour day
   b. 33 Strategies of War
   c. 1990 Clean Air Act
   d. Sherman Antitrust Act

40. An _____ is a practitioner of accountancy, which is the measurement, disclosure or provision of assurance about financial information that helps managers, investors, tax authorities and other decision makers make resource allocation decisions.

The word '_____' is derived from the French 'Compter' which took its origin from the Latin 'Computare'. The word was formerly written in English as 'Accomptant', but in process of time the word, which was always pronounced by dropping the 'p', became gradually changed both in pronunciation and in orthography to its present form.

   a. A4e
   b. A Stake in the Outcome
   c. Accountant
   d. AAAI

Chapter 10. ACCOUNTING, TREASURY, AND FINANCE-MANAGEMENT BEST PRACTICES

41. The _____ is an independent agency of the United States government, established in 1914 by the _____ Act. Its principal mission is the promotion of 'consumer protection' and the elimination and prevention of what regulators perceive to be harmfully 'anti-competitive' business practices, such as coercive monopoly.

The _____ Act was one of President Wilson's major acts against trusts.

   a. 28-hour day
   b. 33 Strategies of War
   c. 1990 Clean Air Act
   d. Federal Trade Commission

42. The _____ of 1914 (15 U.S.C §§ 41-58, as amended) established the Federal Trade Commission (FTC), a bipartisan body of five members appointed by the President of the United States for seven year terms. This Commission was authorized to issue Cease and Desist orders to large corporations to curb unfair trade practices. This Act also gave more flexibility to the US congress for judicial matters.

   a. Comprehensive Environmental Response, Compensation, and Liability Act
   b. Federal Trade Commission Act
   c. Resource Conservation and Recovery Act
   d. Sarbanes-Oxley Act of 2002

43. The _____ is an Act of the 106th United States Congress which repealed part of the Glass-Steagall Act of 1933, opening up competition among banks, securities companies and insurance companies.

   a. 1990 Clean Air Act
   b. 28-hour day
   c. 33 Strategies of War
   d. Gramm-Leach-Bliley Act

Chapter 11. INFORMATION-TECHNOLOGY MANAGEMENT BEST PRACTICES

1. The _____ is a job title for the board level head of information technology within an organization. The _____ typically reports to the chief operations officer or the chief executive officer. In military organizations, they report to the commanding officer or commanding general of the organization.
    a. 33 Strategies of War
    b. 1990 Clean Air Act
    c. Chief information officer
    d. 28-hour day

2. _____ is a structured approach to transitioning individuals, teams, and organizations from a current state to a desired future state. The current definition of _____ includes both organizational _____ processes and individual _____ models, which together are used to manage the people side of change.

A number of models are available for understanding the transitioning of individuals through the phases of _____ and strengthening organizational development initiative in both government and corporate sectors.

    a. 28-hour day
    b. 33 Strategies of War
    c. 1990 Clean Air Act
    d. Change management

3. _____ is, in very basic words, a position a firm occupies against its competitors.

According to Michael Porter, the three methods for creating a sustainable _____ are through:

1. Cost leadership

2. Differentiation

3. Focus (economics)

    a. 28-hour day
    b. 1990 Clean Air Act
    c. Theory Z
    d. Competitive advantage

4. In probability theory, a probability distribution is called _____ if its cumulative distribution function is _____. This is equivalent to saying that for random variables X with the distribution in question, Pr[X = a] = 0 for all real numbers a, i.e.: the probability that X attains the value a is zero, for any number a. If the distribution of X is _____ then X is called a _____ random variable.
    a. Decision tree pruning
    b. Connectionist expert systems
    c. Continuous
    d. Pay Band

5. _____ is a management process whereby delivery (customer valued) processes are constantly evaluated and improved in the light of their efficiency, effectiveness and flexibility.

Some see it as a meta process for most management systems (Business Process Management, Quality Management, Project Management). Deming saw it as part of the 'system' whereby feedback from the process and customer were evaluated against organisational goals.

    a. Sole proprietorship
    b. Critical Success Factor
    c. First-mover advantage
    d. Continuous Improvement Process

Chapter 11. INFORMATION-TECHNOLOGY MANAGEMENT BEST PRACTICES

6. _____ can be considered to have three main components: quality control, quality assurance and quality improvement. _____ is focused not only on product quality, but also the means to achieve it. _____ therefore uses quality assurance and control of processes as well as products to achieve more consistent quality.
   a. Total quality management
   b. 1990 Clean Air Act
   c. 28-hour day
   d. Quality management

7. _____ is a term used in business and Information Technology (through ITIL) to describe the process of capturing a customer's requirements. Specifically, the _____ is a market research technique that produces a detailed set of customer wants and needs, organized into a hierarchical structure, and then prioritized in terms of relative importance and satisfaction with current alternatives. _____ studies typically consist of both qualitative and quantitative research steps.
   a. Business philosophy
   b. Goal setting
   c. Board of governors
   d. Voice of the customer

8. The general definition of an _____ is an evaluation of a person, organization, system, process, project or product. _____s are performed to ascertain the validity and reliability of information; also to provide an assessment of a system's internal control. The goal of an _____ is to express an opinion on the person / organization/system (etc) in question, under evaluation based on work done on a test basis.
   a. Audit committee
   b. A Stake in the Outcome
   c. Internal control
   d. Audit

9. A _____ is a volunteer group composed of workers (or even students), usually under the leadership of their supervisor (but they can elect a team leader), who are trained to identify, analyse and solve work-related problems and present their solutions to management in order to improve the performance of the organization, and motivate and enrich the work of employees. When matured, true _____s become self-managing, having gained the confidence of management. _____s are an alternative to the dehumanising concept of the Division of Labour, where workers or individuals are treated like robots.
   a. Certified in Production and Inventory Management
   b. Competency-based job descriptions
   c. Quality circle
   d. Connectionist expert systems

10. _____ is the process of comparing the cost, cycle time, productivity, or quality of a specific process or method to another that is widely considered to be an industry standard or best practice. Essentially, _____ provides a snapshot of the performance of your business and helps you understand where you are in relation to a particular standard. The result is often a business case for making changes in order to make improvements.
    a. Competitive heterogeneity
    b. Cost leadership
    c. Complementors
    d. Benchmarking

11. _____ is an organization's process of defining its strategy and making decisions on allocating its resources to pursue this strategy, including its capital and people. Various business analysis techniques can be used in _____, including SWOT analysis (Strengths, Weaknesses, Opportunities, and Threats) and PEST analysis (Political, Economic, Social, and Technological analysis) or STEER analysis involving Socio-cultural, Technological, Economic, Ecological, and Regulatory factors and EPISTEL (Environment, Political, Informatic, Social, Technological, Economic and Legal)

Chapter 11. INFORMATION-TECHNOLOGY MANAGEMENT BEST PRACTICES

_____ is the formal consideration of an organization's future course. All _____ deals with at least one of three key questions:

1. 'What do we do?'
2. 'For whom do we do it?'
3. 'How do we excel?'

In business _____, the third question is better phrased 'How can we beat or avoid competition?'. (Bradford and Duncan, page 1.)

a. 33 Strategies of War
c. Strategic planning
b. 1990 Clean Air Act
d. 28-hour day

12. _____ is subcontracting a process, such as product design or manufacturing, to a third-party company. The decision to outsource is often made in the interest of lowering cost or making better use of time and energy costs, redirecting or conserving energy directed at the competencies of a particular business, or to make more efficient use of land, labor, capital, (information) technology and resources. _____ became part of the business lexicon during the 1980s.

a. Operant conditioning
c. Opinion leadership
b. Unemployment insurance
d. Outsourcing

13. A _____ is defined as someone who controls access to something. It also refers to individuals who decide whether a given message will be distributed by a mass medium.

_____s serve several different purposes such as academic admissions, financial advising, and news editing.

a. 1990 Clean Air Act
c. 28-hour day
b. 33 Strategies of War
d. Gatekeeper

14. _____ is an advertisement in which a particular product specifically mentions a competitor by name for the express purpose of showing why the competitor is inferior to the product naming it.

This should not be confused with parody advertisements, where a fictional product is being advertised for the purpose of poking fun at the particular advertisement, nor should it be confused with the use of a coined brand name for the purpose of comparing the product without actually naming an actual competitor. ('Wikipedia tastes better and is less filling than the Encyclopedia Galactica.')

In the 1980s, during what has been referred to as the cola wars, soft-drink manufacturer Pepsi ran a series of advertisements where people, caught on hidden camera, in a blind taste test, chose Pepsi over rival Coca-Cola.

a. 33 Strategies of War
c. Comparative advertising
b. 28-hour day
d. 1990 Clean Air Act

Chapter 11. INFORMATION-TECHNOLOGY MANAGEMENT BEST PRACTICES

15. In economics, _____ is a measure of the relative satisfaction from consumption of various goods and services. Given this measure, one may speak meaningfully of increasing or decreasing _____, and thereby explain economic behavior in terms of attempts to increase one's _____. For illustrative purposes, changes in _____ are sometimes expressed in units called utils.
   a. Ordinal utility
   b. A Stake in the Outcome
   c. Indirect utility function
   d. Utility

16. The _____ is a performance management tool for measuring whether the smaller-scale operational activities of a company are aligned with its larger-scale objectives in terms of vision and strategy.

By focusing not only on financial outcomes but also on the operational, marketing and developmental inputs to these, the _____ helps provide a more comprehensive view of a business, which in turn helps organizations act in their best long-term interests. This tool is also being used to address business response to climate change and greenhouse gas emissions.

   a. Balanced scorecard
   b. Management development
   c. Middle management
   d. Commercial management

17. _____ is a forward looking process for setting goals and regularly checking progress toward achieving those goals. It is a continual feedback process whereby the actual outputs are measured and compared with the desired goals. Any discrepancy or gap is then fed back into changing the inputs of the process, so as to achieve the desired goals or outputs.
   a. 33 Strategies of War
   b. 1990 Clean Air Act
   c. Performance management
   d. 28-hour day

18. _____ or contract administration is the management of contracts made with customers, vendors, partners, or employees. _____ includes negotiating the terms and conditions in contracts and ensuring compliance with the terms and conditions, as well as documenting and agreeing any changes that may arise during its implementation or execution. It can be summarized as the process of systematically and efficiently managing contract creating, execution, and analysis for the purpose of maximizing financial and operational performance and minimizing risk.
   a. 1990 Clean Air Act
   b. World Trade Organization
   c. Network planning and design
   d. Contract management

19. In decision theory and estimation theory, the _____ of an estimator, $\hat{\theta}$, of an unknown parameter of the distribution, θ, is the expected value of the loss function

$$R(\theta, \hat{\theta}) = \mathbb{E}_\theta L(\theta, \hat{\theta}) = \int L(\theta, \hat{\theta}) \, dP_\theta.$$

Chapter 11. INFORMATION-TECHNOLOGY MANAGEMENT BEST PRACTICES

where dP_θ is a probability measure parametrized by θ.

- For a scalar parameter θ and a quadratic loss function,

$$L(\theta, \hat{\theta}) = (\theta - \hat{\theta})^2$$

the _____ function becomes the mean squared error of the estimate,

$$R(\theta, \hat{\theta}) = E_\theta (\theta - \hat{\theta})^2$$

- In density estimation, the unknown parameter is probability density itself. The loss function is typically chosen to be a norm in an appropriate function space. For example, for L^2 norm,

$$L(f, \hat{f}) = \|f - \hat{f}\|_2^2$$

the _____ function becomes the mean integrated squared error

$$R(f, \hat{f}) = E\|f - \hat{f}\|^2$$

a. Financial modeling
c. Risk aversion
b. Linear model
d. Risk

20. _____ is a systematic method to improve the 'value' of goods or products and services by using an examination of function. Value, as defined, is the ratio of function to cost. Value can therefore be increased by either improving the function or reducing the cost.

a. Master production schedule
c. Capacity planning
b. Cellular manufacturing
d. Value engineering

21. _____ refers to planned and systematic production processes that provide confidence in a product's suitability for its intended purpose. Refer to the definition by Merriam-Webster for further information. It is a set of activities intended to ensure that products (goods and/or services) satisfy customer requirements in a systematic, reliable fashion.

a. 28-hour day
c. Risk assessment
b. 1990 Clean Air Act
d. Quality assurance

Chapter 11. INFORMATION-TECHNOLOGY MANAGEMENT BEST PRACTICES

22. _____ is the identification, assessment, and prioritization of risks followed by coordinated and economical application of resources to minimize, monitor, and control the probability and/or impact of unfortunate events.. Risks can come from uncertainty in financial markets, project failures, legal liabilities, credit risk, accidents, natural causes and disasters as well as deliberate attacks from an adversary. Several _____ standards have been developed including the Project Management Institute, the National Institute of Science and Technology, actuarial societies, and ISO standards.

   a. Succession planning
   b. Kanban
   c. Risk management
   d. Trademark

23. In a publicly-held company, an _____ is an operating committee of the Board of Directors, typically charged with oversight of financial reporting and disclosure. Committee members are drawn from members of the Company's board of directors, with a Chairperson selected from among the members. An _____ of a publicly-traded company in the United States is composed of independent and outside directors referred to as non-executive directors, at least one of which is typically a financial expert.

   a. Internal control
   b. Internal auditing
   c. A Stake in the Outcome
   d. Audit committee

24. _____ is a step in a risk management process. _____ is the determination of quantitative or qualitative value of risk related to a concrete situation and a recognized threat (also called hazard.) Quantitative _____ requires calculations of two components of risk: R, the magnitude of the potential loss L, and the probability p, that the loss will occur.

   a. 28-hour day
   b. 1990 Clean Air Act
   c. Quality assurance
   d. Risk assessment

25. A _____ is a set of instructions having the force of a directive, covering those features of operations that lend themselves to a definite or standardized procedure without loss of effectiveness. Standard Operating Policies and Procedures can be effective catalysts to drive performance improvement and improving organizational results.

   a. 1990 Clean Air Act
   b. Longitudinal study
   c. Risk-benefit analysis
   d. Standard operating procedure

26. _____, commonly known as e-commerce, consists of the buying and selling of products or services over electronic systems such as the Internet and other computer networks. The amount of trade conducted electronically has grown extraordinarily with widespread Internet usage. The use of commerce is conducted in this way, spurring and drawing on innovations in electronic funds transfer, supply chain management, Internet marketing, online transaction processing, electronic data interchange (EDI), inventory management systems, and automated data collection systems.

   a. Online shopping
   b. Electronic Commerce
   c. A4e
   d. A Stake in the Outcome

27. The _____ is a concept from business management that was first described and popularized by Michael Porter in his 1985 best-seller, Competitive Advantage: Creating and Sustaining Superior Performance.

A _____ is a chain of activities. Products pass through all activities of the chain in order and at each activity the product gains some value. The chain of activities gives the products more added value than the sum of added values of all activities. It is important not to mix the concept of the _____ with the costs occurring throughout the activities.

Chapter 11. INFORMATION-TECHNOLOGY MANAGEMENT BEST PRACTICES

a. Market development
b. Customer relationship management
c. Value chain
d. Mass marketing

28. _____ refers to the structured transmission of data between organizations by electronic means. It is used to transfer electronic documents from one computer system to another (ie) from one trading partner to another trading partner. It is more than mere E-mail; for instance, organizations might replace bills of lading and even checks with appropriate _____ messages.

a. A Stake in the Outcome
b. Electronic data interchange
c. AAAI
d. A4e

29. _____ is one of the managerial functions like planning, organizing, staffing and directing. It is an important function because it helps to check the errors and to take the corrective action so that deviation from standards are minimized and stated goals of the organization are achieved in desired manner. According to modern concepts, _____ is a foreseeing action whereas earlier concept of _____ was used only when errors were detected. _____ in management means setting standards, measuring actual performance and taking corrective action.

a. Decision tree pruning
b. Schedule of reinforcement
c. Turnover
d. Control

30. A _____ is typically described as a deliberate plan of action to guide decisions and achieve rational outcome(s.) However, the term may also be used to denote what is actually done, even though it is unplanned.

The term may apply to government, private sector organizations and groups, and individuals.

a. 33 Strategies of War
b. 28-hour day
c. 1990 Clean Air Act
d. Policy

31. _____ is a term that refers both to:

- a formal discipline used to help appraise, or assess, the case for a project or proposal, which itself is a process known as project appraisal; and
- an informal approach to making decisions of any kind.

Under both definitions the process involves, whether explicitly or implicitly, weighing the total expected costs against the total expected benefits of one or more actions in order to choose the best or most profitable option. The formal process is often referred to as either CBA (_____) or BCost-benefit analysis

A hallmark of CBA is that all benefits and all costs are expressed in money terms, and are adjusted for the time value of money, so that all flows of benefits and flows of project costs over time (which tend to occur at different points in time) are expressed on a common basis in terms of their 'present value.' Closely related, but slightly different, formal techniques include Cost-effectiveness analysis, Economic impact analysis, Fiscal impact analysis and Social Return on Investment(SROI) analysis. The latter builds upon the logic of _____, but differs in that it is explicitly designed to inform the practical decision-making of enterprise managers and investors focused on optimising their social and environmental impacts.

a. Gittins index
b. Cost-benefit analysis
c. Decision engineering
d. Kepner-Tregoe

32. _____ is the process by which an organization deals with any major unpredictable event that threatens to harm the organization, its stakeholders, or the general public. Three elements are common to most definitions of crisis: (a) a threat to the organization, (b) the element of surprise, and (c) a short decision time.

Whereas risk management involves assessing potential threats and finding the best ways to avoid those threats, _____ involves dealing with the disasters after they have occurred.

a. Business value
b. Crisis management
c. Capability management
d. C-A-K-E

33. _____ is a concept in ethics with several meanings. It is often used synonymously with such concepts as responsibility, answerability, enforcement, blameworthiness, liability and other terms associated with the expectation of account-giving. As an aspect of governance, it has been central to discussions related to problems in both the public and private (corporation) worlds.

a. Usury
b. A Stake in the Outcome
c. A4e
d. Accountability

34. A _____ is a set of exclusive rights granted by a state to an inventor or his assignee for a limited period of time in exchange for a disclosure of an invention.

The procedure for granting _____s, the requirements placed on the _____ee and the extent of the exclusive rights vary widely between countries according to national laws and international agreements. Typically, however, a _____ application must include one or more claims defining the invention which must be new, inventive, and useful or industrially applicable.

a. Federal Trade Commission Act
b. Labor Management Reporting and Disclosure Act
c. Food, Drug, and Cosmetic Act
d. Patent

35. The _____ of 2002 (Pub.L. 107-204, 116 Stat. 745, enacted July 30, 2002), also known as the Public Company Accounting Reform and Investor Protection Act of 2002 and commonly called Sarbanes-Oxley, Sarbox or SOX, is a United States federal law enacted on July 30, 2002, as a reaction to a number of major corporate and accounting scandals including those affecting Enron, Tyco International, Adelphia, Peregrine Systems and WorldCom.

a. Fair Labor Standards Act
b. Letter of credit
c. Sarbanes-Oxley Act of 2002
d. Sarbanes-Oxley Act

36. _____ generally refers to a list of all planned expenses and revenues. It is a plan for saving and spending. A _____ is an important concept in microeconomics, which uses a _____ line to illustrate the trade-offs between two or more goods.

a. Budget
b. 1990 Clean Air Act
c. 33 Strategies of War
d. 28-hour day

Chapter 11. INFORMATION-TECHNOLOGY MANAGEMENT BEST PRACTICES

37. The _____ of 1977 (15 U.S.C. §§ 78dd-1, et seq.) is a United States federal law known primarily for two of its main provisions, one that addresses accounting transparency requirements under the Securities Exchange Act of 1934 and another concerning bribery of foreign officials.

    a. Meritor Savings Bank v. Vinson
    b. Foreign Corrupt Practices Act
    c. Social Security Act of 1965
    d. Limited liability

38. The _____ is a United States federal law that provides for extended criminal penalties and a civil cause of action for acts performed as part of an ongoing criminal organization. RICO was enacted by section 901(a) of the Organized Crime Control Act of 1970 (Pub.L. 91-452, 84 Stat.

    a. Business valuation
    b. Negligence in employment
    c. Minimum wage law
    d. Racketeer Influenced and Corrupt Organizations Act

39. The _____ is an Act of the 106th United States Congress which repealed part of the Glass-Steagall Act of 1933, opening up competition among banks, securities companies and insurance companies.

    a. 33 Strategies of War
    b. Gramm-Leach-Bliley Act
    c. 1990 Clean Air Act
    d. 28-hour day

40. An _____ is a practitioner of accountancy, which is the measurement, disclosure or provision of assurance about financial information that helps managers, investors, tax authorities and other decision makers make resource allocation decisions.

The word '_____' is derived from the French 'Compter' which took its origin from the Latin 'Computare'. The word was formerly written in English as 'Accomptant', but in process of time the word, which was always pronounced by dropping the 'p', became gradually changed both in pronunciation and in orthography to its present form.

    a. Accountant
    b. AAAI
    c. A4e
    d. A Stake in the Outcome

41. The _____ is an international, independent, not-for-profit organization dedicated to benchmarking and identifying good practices in information security. It was established in 1989 as the European Security Forum and expanded its mission and membership in the 1990s. It now includes hundreds of members, including a large number of Fortune 500 companies, from North America, Asia, and other locations around the world.

    a. A Stake in the Outcome
    b. Information Security Forum
    c. A4e
    d. AAAI

Chapter 12. INTERNATIONAL-BUSINESS MANAGEMENT BEST PRACTICES

1. _____ is subcontracting a process, such as product design or manufacturing, to a third-party company. The decision to outsource is often made in the interest of lowering cost or making better use of time and energy costs, redirecting or conserving energy directed at the competencies of a particular business, or to make more efficient use of land, labor, capital, (information) technology and resources. _____ became part of the business lexicon during the 1980s.

   a. Operant conditioning
   b. Unemployment insurance
   c. Opinion leadership
   d. Outsourcing

2. _____ in its literal sense is the process of transformation of local or regional phenomena into global ones. It can be described as a process by which the people of the world are unified into a single society and function together.

   This process is a combination of economic, technological, sociocultural and political forces.

   a. Globalization
   b. Histogram
   c. Cost Management
   d. Collaborative Planning, Forecasting and Replenishment

3. In probability theory, a probability distribution is called _____ if its cumulative distribution function is _____. This is equivalent to saying that for random variables X with the distribution in question, Pr[X = a] = 0 for all real numbers a, i.e.: the probability that X attains the value a is zero, for any number a. If the distribution of X is _____ then X is called a _____ random variable.

   a. Decision tree pruning
   b. Continuous
   c. Pay Band
   d. Connectionist expert systems

4. _____ is a management process whereby delivery (customer valued) processes are constantly evaluated and improved in the light of their efficiency, effectiveness and flexibility.

   Some see it as a meta process for most management systems (Business Process Management, Quality Management, Project Management). Deming saw it as part of the 'system' whereby feedback from the process and customer were evaluated against organisational goals.

   a. Critical Success Factor
   b. Sole proprietorship
   c. First-mover advantage
   d. Continuous Improvement Process

5. _____ is exchange of capital, goods, and services across international borders or territories. In most countries, it represents a significant share of gross domestic product (GDP.) While _____ has been present throughout much of history, its economic, social, and political importance has been on the rise in recent centuries.

   a. A4e
   b. International trade
   c. A Stake in the Outcome
   d. AAAI

6. _____ are legal property rights over creations of the mind, both artistic and commercial, and the corresponding fields of law. Under _____ law, owners are granted certain exclusive rights to a variety of intangible assets, such as musical, literary, and artistic works; ideas, discoveries and inventions; and words, phrases, symbols, and designs. Common types of _____ include copyrights, trademarks, patents, industrial design rights and trade secrets.

   a. Unemployment Action Center
   b. Intent
   c. Equal Pay Act
   d. Intellectual property

Chapter 12. INTERNATIONAL-BUSINESS MANAGEMENT BEST PRACTICES

7. _____ plant, and equipment, is a term used in accountancy for assets and property which cannot easily be converted into cash. This can be compared with current assets such as cash or bank accounts, which are described as liquid assets. In most cases, only tangible assets are referred to as fixed.

   a. 28-hour day
   b. 1990 Clean Air Act
   c. Fixed asset
   d. 33 Strategies of War

8. A _____ is a set of exclusive rights granted by a state to an inventor or his assignee for a limited period of time in exchange for a disclosure of an invention.

   The procedure for granting _____s, the requirements placed on the _____ee and the extent of the exclusive rights vary widely between countries according to national laws and international agreements. Typically, however, a _____ application must include one or more claims defining the invention which must be new, inventive, and useful or industrially applicable.

   a. Labor Management Reporting and Disclosure Act
   b. Federal Trade Commission Act
   c. Food, Drug, and Cosmetic Act
   d. Patent

9. A _____ is typically described as a deliberate plan of action to guide decisions and achieve rational outcome(s.) However, the term may also be used to denote what is actually done, even though it is unplanned.

   The term may apply to government, private sector organizations and groups, and individuals.

   a. 1990 Clean Air Act
   b. 28-hour day
   c. 33 Strategies of War
   d. Policy

10. A _____ is a formula, practice, process, design, instrument, pattern by which a business can obtain an economic advantage over competitors or customers. In some jurisdictions, such secrets are referred to as 'confidential information' or 'classified information'.

    The precise language by which a _____ is defined varies by jurisdiction (as do the particular types of information that are subject to _____ protection.)

    a. Right to Financial Privacy Act
    b. Federal Trade Commission Act
    c. Business valuation
    d. Trade secret

11. A _____ is a distinctive sign or indicator used by an individual, business organization, or other legal entity to identify that the products and/or services to consumers with which the _____ appears originate from a unique source and to distinguish its products or services from those of other entities.

    a. Succession planning
    b. Kanban
    c. Virtual team
    d. Trademark

12. _____ is an advertisement in which a particular product specifically mentions a competitor by name for the express purpose of showing why the competitor is inferior to the product naming it.

This should not be confused with parody advertisements, where a fictional product is being advertised for the purpose of poking fun at the particular advertisement, nor should it be confused with the use of a coined brand name for the purpose of comparing the product without actually naming an actual competitor. ('Wikipedia tastes better and is less filling than the Encyclopedia Galactica.')

In the 1980s, during what has been referred to as the cola wars, soft-drink manufacturer Pepsi ran a series of advertisements where people, caught on hidden camera, in a blind taste test, chose Pepsi over rival Coca-Cola.

    a. 33 Strategies of War
    b. Comparative advertising
    c. 1990 Clean Air Act
    d. 28-hour day

13. _____ refers to the methods of practicing and using another person's business philosophy. The franchisor grants the independent operator the right to distribute its products, techniques, and trademarks for a percentage of gross monthly sales and a royalty fee. Various tangibles and intangibles such as national or international advertising, training, and other support services are commonly made available by the franchisor.

    a. ServiceMaster
    b. 1990 Clean Air Act
    c. 28-hour day
    d. Franchising

14. In decision theory and estimation theory, the _____ of an estimator, $\hat{\theta}$, of an unknown parameter of the distribution, θ, is the expected value of the loss function

$$R(\theta, \hat{\theta}) = \mathbb{E}_\theta L(\theta, \hat{\theta}) = \int L(\theta, \hat{\theta})\, dP_\theta.$$

Chapter 12. INTERNATIONAL-BUSINESS MANAGEMENT BEST PRACTICES

where dP_θ is a probability measure parametrized by θ.

- For a scalar parameter θ and a quadratic loss function,

$$L(\theta, \hat{\theta}) = (\theta - \hat{\theta})^2$$

the _____ function becomes the mean squared error of the estimate,

$$R(\theta, \hat{\theta}) = E_\theta (\theta - \hat{\theta})^2$$

- In density estimation, the unknown parameter is probability density itself. The loss function is typically chosen to be a norm in an appropriate function space. For example, for L^2 norm,

$$L(f, \hat{f}) = \|f - \hat{f}\|_2^2$$

the _____ function becomes the mean integrated squared error

$$R(f, \hat{f}) = E\|f - \hat{f}\|^2$$

a. Financial modeling
b. Linear model
c. Risk aversion
d. Risk

15. _____ is the identification, assessment, and prioritization of risks followed by coordinated and economical application of resources to minimize, monitor, and control the probability and/or impact of unfortunate events.. Risks can come from uncertainty in financial markets, project failures, legal liabilities, credit risk, accidents, natural causes and disasters as well as deliberate attacks from an adversary. Several _____ standards have been developed including the Project Management Institute, the National Institute of Science and Technology, actuarial societies, and ISO standards.
    a. Risk management
    b. Succession planning
    c. Trademark
    d. Kanban

16. The general definition of an _____ is an evaluation of a person, organization, system, process, project or product. _____s are performed to ascertain the validity and reliability of information; also to provide an assessment of a system's internal control. The goal of an _____ is to express an opinion on the person / organization/system (etc) in question, under evaluation based on work done on a test basis.
    a. A Stake in the Outcome
    b. Audit
    c. Audit committee
    d. Internal control

Chapter 12. INTERNATIONAL-BUSINESS MANAGEMENT BEST PRACTICES

17. In a publicly-held company, an _____ is an operating committee of the Board of Directors, typically charged with oversight of financial reporting and disclosure. Committee members are drawn from members of the Company's board of directors, with a Chairperson selected from among the members. An _____ of a publicly-traded company in the United States is composed of independent and outside directors referred to as non-executive directors, at least one of which is typically a financial expert.

   a. Audit committee
   b. Internal auditing
   c. Internal control
   d. A Stake in the Outcome

18. The _____ or gross domestic income (GDI), a basic measure of an economy's economic performance, is the market value of all final goods and services made within the borders of a nation in a year. _____ can be defined in three ways, all of which are conceptually identical. First, it is equal to the total expenditures for all final goods and services produced within the country in a stipulated period of time (usually a 365-day year).

   a. Productivity management
   b. Gross domestic product
   c. Human capital
   d. Perfect competition

19. A _____ is the belief that there is a technique, method, process, activity, incentive or reward that is more effective at delivering a particular outcome than any other technique, method, process, etc. The idea is that with proper processes, checks, and testing, a desired outcome can be delivered with fewer problems and unforeseen complications. _____s can also be defined as the most efficient (least amount of effort) and effective (best results) way of accomplishing a task, based on repeatable procedures that have proven themselves over time for large numbers of people.

   a. Hierarchical organization
   b. Design management
   c. Fix it twice
   d. Best practice

20. _____ generally refers to a list of all planned expenses and revenues. It is a plan for saving and spending. A _____ is an important concept in microeconomics, which uses a _____ line to illustrate the trade-offs between two or more goods.

   a. 1990 Clean Air Act
   b. 33 Strategies of War
   c. Budget
   d. 28-hour day

21. _____ is the planning process used to determine whether a firm's long term investments such as new machinery, replacement machinery, new plants, new products, and research development projects are worth pursuing. It is budget for major capital, or investment, expenditures.

Many formal methods are used in _____, including the techniques such as

- Net present value
- Profitability index
- Internal rate of return
- Modified Internal Rate of Return
- Equivalent annuity

These methods use the incremental cash flows from each potential investment, or project. Techniques based on accounting earnings and accounting rules are sometimes used - though economists consider this to be improper - such as the accounting rate of return, and 'return on investment.' Simplified and hybrid methods are used as well, such as payback period and discounted payback period.

Chapter 12. INTERNATIONAL-BUSINESS MANAGEMENT BEST PRACTICES

a. Gross profit
b. Restricted stock
c. Gross profit margin
d. Capital budgeting

22. The _____ of 1988 is an act passed by the United States Congress and signed into law by President Ronald Reagan.

During the 1970s, the American Trade surplus slowly diminished and morphed in to an increasing deficit. As the deficit increased through the 80's, the blame fell on the tariffs placed on American products by foreign countries, and the lack of similar tariffs on imports into the United States.

a. A Stake in the Outcome
b. AAAI
c. A4e
d. Omnibus Foreign Trade and Competitiveness Act

23. _____ is a type of trade policy that allows traders to act and transact without interference from government. Thus, the policy permits trading partners mutual gains from trade, with goods and services produced according to the theory of comparative advantage.

Under a _____ policy, prices are a reflection of true supply and demand, and are the sole determinant of resource allocation.

a. Free Trade
b. 28-hour day
c. 1990 Clean Air Act
d. 33 Strategies of War

24. _____ is a designated group of countries that have agreed to eliminate tariffs, quotas and preferences on most (if not all) goods and services traded between them. It can be considered the second stage of economic integration. Countries choose this kind of economic integration form if their economical structures are complementary.

a. 1990 Clean Air Act
b. Free trade area
c. 28-hour day
d. 33 Strategies of War

25. The _____ is a trilateral trade bloc in North America created by the governments of the United States, Canada, and Mexico. The agreement creating the trade bloc came into force on January 1, 1994. It superseded the Canada-United States Free Trade Agreement between the U.S. and Canada.

a. Career portfolios
b. Trade union
c. North American Free Trade Agreement
d. Business war game

26. The _____ of 1990 (ADA) is the short title of United States (Pub.L. 101-336, 104 Stat. 327, enacted July 26, 1990), codified at 42 U.S.C. § 12101 et seq. It was signed into law on July 26, 1990, by President George H. W. Bush, and later amended with changes effective January 1, 2009. The ADA is a wide-ranging civil rights law that prohibits, under certain circumstances, discrimination based on disability. It affords similar protections against discrimination to Americans with disabilities as the Civil Rights Act of 1964,

a. Australian labour law
b. Employment discrimination
c. Equal Pay Act of 1963
d. Americans with Disabilities Act

Chapter 12. INTERNATIONAL-BUSINESS MANAGEMENT BEST PRACTICES

27. _____ is a contract between two parties, one being the employer and the other being the employee. An employee may be defined as: 'A person in the service of another under any contract of hire, express or implied, oral or written, where the employer has the power or right to control and direct the employee in the material details of how the work is to be performed.' Black's Law Dictionary page 471 (5th ed. 1979.)

   a. Exit interview
   b. Employment rate
   c. Employment
   d. Employment counsellor

28. _____ refers to discriminatory employment practices such as bias in hiring, promotion, job assignment, termination, and compensation, and various types of harassment.

In many countries, laws prohibit employers from discriminating on the basis of race, color, sex, religion, national origin, physical or mental disability, or age. There is also a growing body of law preventing or occasionally justifying _____ based on sexual orientation or gender identity.

   a. Employment discrimination
   b. Employee Retirement Income Security Act
   c. Extra time
   d. Invitee

29. The _____ of 1977 (15 U.S.C. §§ 78dd-1, et seq.) is a United States federal law known primarily for two of its main provisions, one that addresses accounting transparency requirements under the Securities Exchange Act of 1934 and another concerning bribery of foreign officials.

   a. Social Security Act of 1965
   b. Limited liability
   c. Foreign Corrupt Practices Act
   d. Meritor Savings Bank v. Vinson

Chapter 13. PROJECT-MANAGEMENT BEST PRACTICES

1. _____ refers to the movement of cash into or out of a business or financial product. It is usually measured during a specified, finite period of time. Measurement of _____ can be used

- to determine a project's rate of return or value. The time of _____s into and out of projects are used as inputs in financial models such as internal rate of return, and net present value.
- to determine problems with a business's liquidity. Being profitable does not necessarily mean being liquid. A company can fail because of a shortage of cash, even while profitable.
- as an alternate measure of a business's profits when it is believed that accrual accounting concepts do not represent economic realities. For example, a company may be notionally profitable but generating little operational cash (as may be the case for a company that barters its products rather than selling for cash.) In such a case, the company may be deriving additional operating cash by issuing shares evaluating default risk, re-investment requirements, etc.

_____ is a generic term used differently depending on the context. It may be defined by users for their own purposes.

a. Sweat equity
b. Cash flow
c. Gross profit
d. Gross profit margin

2. _____ is the discipline of planning, organizing and managing resources to bring about the successful completion of specific project goals and objectives. It is often closely related to and sometimes conflated with Program management.

A project is a finite endeavor--having specific start and completion dates--undertaken to meet particular goals and objectives, usually to bring about beneficial change or added value.

a. Project engineer
b. Project management
c. Precedence diagram
d. Work package

3. A _____ is a professional in the field of project management. _____s can have the responsibility of the planning, execution, and closing of any project, typically relating to construction industry, architecture, computer networking, telecommunications or software development.

Many other fields in the production, design and service industries also have _____s.

a. Work package
b. Project manager
c. Project engineer
d. Project management

4. _____ generally refers to a list of all planned expenses and revenues. It is a plan for saving and spending. A _____ is an important concept in microeconomics, which uses a _____ line to illustrate the trade-offs between two or more goods.

a. 28-hour day
b. 33 Strategies of War
c. 1990 Clean Air Act
d. Budget

5. In economics, business, retail, and accounting, a _____ is the value of money that has been used up to produce something, and hence is not available for use anymore. In economics, a _____ is an alternative that is given up as a result of a decision. In business, the _____ may be one of acquisition, in which case the amount of money expended to acquire it is counted as _____.

Chapter 13. PROJECT-MANAGEMENT BEST PRACTICES

a. Cost
b. Fixed costs
c. Cost overrun
d. Cost allocation

6. A _____ in project management and systems engineering, is a tool used to define and group a project's discrete work elements (or tasks) in a way that helps organize and define the total work scope of the project.

A _____ element may be a product, data, a service, or any combination. A _____ also provides the necessary framework for detailed cost estimating and control along with providing guidance for schedule development and control.

a. 33 Strategies of War
b. 1990 Clean Air Act
c. 28-hour day
d. Work breakdown structure

7. _____ is the process whereby companies use cost accounting to report or control the various costs of doing business.

_____ generally describes the approaches and activities of managers in short run and long run planning and control decisions that increase value for customers and lower costs of products and services.

a. Missing completely at random
b. Strict liability
c. Genbutsu
d. Cost management

8. _____ refers to a range of skills, tools, and techniques used to manage time when accomplishing specific tasks, projects and goals. This set encompass a wide scope of activities, and these include planning, allocating, setting goals, delegation, analysis of time spent, monitoring, organizing, scheduling, and prioritizing. Initially _____ referred to just business or work activities, but eventually the term broadened to include personal activities also.

a. Cash cow
b. Formula for Change
c. Voice of the customer
d. Time management

9. _____ is an increasingly broadening term with which an organization, or other human system describes the combination of traditionally administrative personnel functions with acquisition and application of skills, knowledge and experience, Employee Relations and resource planning at various levels. The field draws upon concepts developed in Industrial/Organizational Psychology and System Theory. _____ has at least two related interpretations depending on context. The original usage derives from political economy and economics, where it was traditionally called labor, one of four factors of production although this perspective is changing as a function of new and ongoing research into more strategic approaches at national levels. This first usage is used more in terms of '_____ development', and can go beyond just organizations to the level of nations . The more traditional usage within corporations and businesses refers to the individuals within a firm or agency, and to the portion of the organization that deals with hiring, firing, training, and other personnel issues, typically referred to as '_____ management'.

a. Human resources
b. Progressive discipline
c. Human resource management
d. Bradford Factor

10. _____ can be considered to have three main components: quality control, quality assurance and quality improvement. _____ is focused not only on product quality, but also the means to achieve it. _____ therefore uses quality assurance and control of processes as well as products to achieve more consistent quality.

Chapter 13. PROJECT-MANAGEMENT BEST PRACTICES

a. 1990 Clean Air Act
b. 28-hour day
c. Quality management
d. Total quality management

11. _____ is a business management strategy, initially implemented by Motorola, that today enjoys widespread application in many sectors of industry.

_____ seeks to improve the quality of process outputs by identifying and removing the causes of defects (errors) and variation in manufacturing and business processes. It uses a set of quality management methods, including statistical methods, and creates a special infrastructure of people within the organization ('Black Belts' etc.)

a. Production line
b. Theory of constraints
c. Takt time
d. Six Sigma

12. The general definition of an _____ is an evaluation of a person, organization, system, process, project or product. _____s are performed to ascertain the validity and reliability of information; also to provide an assessment of a system's internal control. The goal of an _____ is to express an opinion on the person / organization/system (etc) in question, under evaluation based on work done on a test basis.

a. Audit committee
b. Internal control
c. A Stake in the Outcome
d. Audit

13. A _____ is the belief that there is a technique, method, process, activity, incentive or reward that is more effective at delivering a particular outcome than any other technique, method, process, etc. The idea is that with proper processes, checks, and testing, a desired outcome can be delivered with fewer problems and unforeseen complications. _____s can also be defined as the most efficient (least amount of effort) and effective (best results) way of accomplishing a task, based on repeatable procedures that have proven themselves over time for large numbers of people.

a. Fix it twice
b. Design management
c. Hierarchical organization
d. Best practice

14. In decision theory and estimation theory, the _____ of an estimator, $\hat{\theta}$, of an unknown parameter of the distribution, θ, is the expected value of the loss function

$$R(\theta, \hat{\theta}) = \mathbb{E}_\theta L(\theta, \hat{\theta}) = \int L(\theta, \hat{\theta})\, dP_\theta.$$

where dP_θ is a probability measure parametrized by θ.

- For a scalar parameter θ and a quadratic loss function,

$$L(\theta, \hat{\theta}) = (\theta - \hat{\theta})^2$$

the _____ function becomes the mean squared error of the estimate,

$$R(\theta, \hat{\theta}) = E_\theta (\theta - \hat{\theta})^2$$

- In density estimation, the unknown parameter is probability density itself. The loss function is typically chosen to be a norm in an appropriate function space. For example, for L^2 norm,

$$L(f, \hat{f}) = \|f - \hat{f}\|_2^2$$

the _____ function becomes the mean integrated squared error

$$R(f, \hat{f}) = E\|f - \hat{f}\|^2$$

a. Financial modeling
c. Linear model
b. Risk aversion
d. Risk

15. _____ is the identification, assessment, and prioritization of risks followed by coordinated and economical application of resources to minimize, monitor, and control the probability and/or impact of unfortunate events.. Risks can come from uncertainty in financial markets, project failures, legal liabilities, credit risk, accidents, natural causes and disasters as well as deliberate attacks from an adversary. Several _____ standards have been developed including the Project Management Institute, the National Institute of Science and Technology, actuarial societies, and ISO standards.
   a. Trademark
   c. Risk management
   b. Succession planning
   d. Kanban

16. In a publicly-held company, an _____ is an operating committee of the Board of Directors, typically charged with oversight of financial reporting and disclosure. Committee members are drawn from members of the Company's board of directors, with a Chairperson selected from among the members. An _____ of a publicly-traded company in the United States is composed of independent and outside directors referred to as non-executive directors, at least one of which is typically a financial expert.
   a. A Stake in the Outcome
   c. Internal control
   b. Internal auditing
   d. Audit committee

Chapter 13. PROJECT-MANAGEMENT BEST PRACTICES

17. _____ is one of the managerial functions like planning, organizing, staffing and directing. It is an important function because it helps to check the errors and to take the corrective action so that deviation from standards are minimized and stated goals of the organization are achieved in desired manner. According to modern concepts, _____ is a foreseeing action whereas earlier concept of _____ was used only when errors were detected. _____ in management means setting standards, measuring actual performance and taking corrective action.

   a. Schedule of reinforcement
   b. Control
   c. Turnover
   d. Decision tree pruning

18. In accounting and auditing, _____ is defined as a process effected by an organization's structure, work and authority flows, people and management information systems, designed to help the organization accomplish specific goals or objectives. It is a means by which an organization's resources are directed, monitored, and measured. It plays an important role in preventing and detecting fraud and protecting the organization's resources, both physical (e.g., machinery and property) and intangible (e.g., reputation or intellectual property such as trademarks.)

   a. Internal auditing
   b. A Stake in the Outcome
   c. Internal control
   d. Audit committee

19. _____ is the acquisition of goods and/or services at the best possible total cost of ownership, in the right quality and quantity, at the right time, in the right place and from the right source for the direct benefit or use of corporations, individuals generally via a contract. Simple _____ may involve nothing more than repeat purchasing. Complex _____ could involve finding long term partners - or even 'co-destiny' suppliers that might fundamentally commit one organization to another.

   a. Golden parachute
   b. Sole proprietorship
   c. Psychological pricing
   d. Procurement

20.

The terms _____ and positive action refer to policies that take race, ethnicity, or gender into consideration in an attempt to promote equal opportunity. The focus of such policies ranges from employment and education to public contracting and health programs. The impetus towards _____ is twofold: to maximize diversity in all levels of society, along with its presumed benefits, and to redress perceived disadvantages due to overt, institutional, or involuntary discrimination.

   a. Affiliation
   b. Abraham Harold Maslow
   c. Affirmative action
   d. Adam Smith

21. The _____ of 1990 (ADA) is the short title of United States (Pub.L. 101-336, 104 Stat. 327, enacted July 26, 1990), codified at 42 U.S.C. § 12101 et seq. It was signed into law on July 26, 1990, by President George H. W. Bush, and later amended with changes effective January 1, 2009. The ADA is a wide-ranging civil rights law that prohibits, under certain circumstances, discrimination based on disability. It affords similar protections against discrimination to Americans with disabilities as the Civil Rights Act of 1964,

   a. Australian labour law
   b. Equal Pay Act of 1963
   c. Employment discrimination
   d. Americans with Disabilities Act

Chapter 13. PROJECT-MANAGEMENT BEST PRACTICES

22. The _____ of 1985 is a law passed by the U.S. Congress and signed by President Reagan that, among other things, mandates an insurance program giving some employees the ability to continue health insurance coverage after leaving employment. _____ includes amendments to the Employee Retirement Income Security Act of 1974 (ERISA.) The law deals with a great variety of subjects, such as tobacco price supports, railroads, private pension plans, disability insurance, and the postal service, but it is perhaps best known for Title X, which amends the Internal Revenue Code to deny income tax deductions to employers for contributions to a group health plan unless such plan meets certain continuing coverage requirements.

   a. 28-hour day
   b. 33 Strategies of War
   c. 1990 Clean Air Act
   d. Consolidated Omnibus Budget Reconciliation Act

23. The _____ of 1977 (15 U.S.C. §§ 78dd-1, et seq.) is a United States federal law known primarily for two of its main provisions, one that addresses accounting transparency requirements under the Securities Exchange Act of 1934 and another concerning bribery of foreign officials.

   a. Limited liability
   b. Meritor Savings Bank v. Vinson
   c. Social Security Act of 1965
   d. Foreign Corrupt Practices Act

24. _____ is a concept in ethics with several meanings. It is often used synonymously with such concepts as responsibility, answerability, enforcement, blameworthiness, liability and other terms associated with the expectation of account-giving. As an aspect of governance, it has been central to discussions related to problems in both the public and private (corporation) worlds.

   a. Accountability
   b. A4e
   c. Usury
   d. A Stake in the Outcome

25. _____ is the term used to refer to the standard framework of guidelines for financial accounting used in any given jurisdiction. _____ includes the standards, conventions, and rules accountants follow in recording and summarizing transactions, and in the preparation of financial statements.

Financial accounting is information that must be assembled and reported objectively.

   a. Net income
   b. Treasury stock
   c. Depreciation
   d. Generally accepted accounting principles

26. _____ is a cross-disciplinary area concerned with protecting the safety, health and welfare of people engaged in work or employment. The goal of all _____ programs is to foster a work free safe environment. As a secondary effect, it may also protect co-workers, family members, employers, customers, suppliers, nearby communities, and other members of the public who are impacted by the workplace environment.

   a. A4e
   b. AAAI
   c. A Stake in the Outcome
   d. Occupational Safety and Health

27. The _____ is the primary federal law which governs occupational health and safety in the private sector and federal government in the United States. It was enacted by Congress in 1970 and was signed by President Richard Nixon on December 29, 1970. Its main goal is to ensure that employers provide employees with an environment free from recognized hazards, such as exposure to toxic chemicals, excessive noise levels, mechanical dangers, heat or cold stress, or unsanitary conditions.

Chapter 13. PROJECT-MANAGEMENT BEST PRACTICES

a. United States Department of Justice
b. Unemployment Action Center
c. Unemployment and Farm Relief Act
d. Occupational Safety and Health Act

28. The _____ is a non-profit professional organization with the purpose of advancing the state-of-the-art of project management. The company is a professional association for the project management profession.

The _____ Inc.

a. 28-hour day
b. 1990 Clean Air Act
c. 33 Strategies of War
d. Project Management Institute

29. _____ is an advertisement in which a particular product specifically mentions a competitor by name for the express purpose of showing why the competitor is inferior to the product naming it.

This should not be confused with parody advertisements, where a fictional product is being advertised for the purpose of poking fun at the particular advertisement, nor should it be confused with the use of a coined brand name for the purpose of comparing the product without actually naming an actual competitor. ('Wikipedia tastes better and is less filling than the Encyclopedia Galactica.')

In the 1980s, during what has been referred to as the cola wars, soft-drink manufacturer Pepsi ran a series of advertisements where people, caught on hidden camera, in a blind taste test, chose Pepsi over rival Coca-Cola.

a. 33 Strategies of War
b. 1990 Clean Air Act
c. 28-hour day
d. Comparative advertising

30. A _____ or business method is a collection of related, structured activities or tasks that produce a specific service or product (serve a particular goal) for a particular customer or customers. It often can be visualized with a flowchart as a sequence of activities.

There are three types of _____ es:

1. Management processes, the processes that govern the operation of a system. Typical management processes include 'Corporate Governance' and 'Strategic Management'.
2. Operational processes, processes that constitute the core business and create the primary value stream. Typical operational processes are Purchasing, Manufacturing, Marketing, and Sales.
3. Supporting processes, which support the core processes. Examples include Accounting, Recruitment, Technical support.

A _____ begins with a customer's need and ends with a customer's need fulfillment. Process oriented organizations break down the barriers of structural departments and try to avoid functional silos.

a. 33 Strategies of War
b. 28-hour day
c. 1990 Clean Air Act
d. Business process

31. In management accounting, _____ establishes budget and actual cost of operations, processes, departments or product and the analysis of variances, profitability or social use of funds. Managers use _____ to support decision-making to cut a company's costs and improve profitability. As a form of management accounting, _____ need not follow standards such as GAAP, because its primary use is for internal managers, rather than outside users, and what to compute is instead decided pragmatically.

   a. Cost accounting
   b. Transaction cost
   c. Quality costs
   d. Marginal cost

ANSWER KEY

Chapter 1
1. d	2. a	3. d	4. c	5. d	6. d	7. d	8. d	9. c	10. d
11. a	12. d	13. d	14. d	15. b	16. d	17. b	18. d	19. a	20. a
21. a	22. d	23. d	24. d	25. d	26. d	27. d	28. b	29. b	30. a
31. c	32. d	33. d	34. d	35. a	36. a	37. a	38. d		

Chapter 2
1. c	2. a	3. d	4. b	5. d	6. d	7. d	8. d	9. d	10. a
11. a	12. d	13. d	14. a	15. b	16. c	17. a	18. c	19. d	20. d
21. d	22. b	23. d	24. d	25. d	26. d	27. d	28. a	29. a	30. d
31. d	32. d	33. c	34. d	35. c	36. d	37. d	38. d	39. a	40. d
41. d	42. d	43. d	44. b	45. a	46. c	47. a	48. d	49. c	50. b
51. d	52. d	53. b	54. b	55. b	56. d	57. d	58. d	59. d	60. d
61. d	62. b	63. a	64. b	65. d	66. d	67. d	68. d	69. b	70. a
71. d	72. d	73. b	74. c	75. b	76. d	77. d	78. b	79. d	80. d
81. b	82. a	83. d	84. a	85. c	86. a	87. d	88. d	89. b	

Chapter 3
1. a	2. d	3. b	4. c	5. a	6. d	7. b	8. d	9. b	10. c
11. d	12. d	13. c	14. d	15. c	16. d	17. d	18. c	19. d	20. a
21. c	22. b	23. b	24. a	25. d	26. b	27. a	28. a	29. d	30. a
31. a	32. d	33. d	34. d	35. d	36. d	37. d	38. c	39. d	40. b

Chapter 4
1. d	2. d	3. d	4. d	5. c	6. a	7. a	8. b	9. d	10. a
11. a	12. d	13. d	14. a	15. d	16. d	17. a	18. b	19. b	20. c
21. c	22. c	23. d	24. a	25. d	26. b	27. d	28. c	29. b	30. d
31. b	32. d	33. a	34. d	35. d	36. b	37. d	38. d		

Chapter 5
1. d	2. a	3. c	4. d	5. a	6. a	7. d	8. d	9. d	10. d
11. d	12. b	13. d	14. d	15. d	16. d	17. d	18. b	19. d	20. d
21. c	22. a	23. c	24. a	25. c	26. a	27. a	28. d	29. d	30. c
31. d	32. d	33. d	34. d	35. c	36. d	37. d	38. b	39. c	40. d
41. a	42. a	43. d	44. c	45. c	46. a	47. b	48. a	49. d	

Chapter 6
1. d	2. b	3. d	4. a	5. c	6. d	7. b	8. b	9. c	10. a
11. b	12. a	13. c	14. d	15. d	16. c	17. d	18. b	19. a	20. b
21. b	22. d	23. b	24. a	25. a	26. a	27. d	28. a	29. a	30. c
31. d	32. b	33. a	34. c	35. d	36. d	37. c	38. d	39. d	40. b
41. a	42. d	43. d	44. d	45. a	46. a	47. a			

Chapter 7

1. a	2. d	3. a	4. b	5. d	6. d	7. c	8. a	9. d	10. d
11. d	12. d	13. c	14. b	15. d	16. d	17. d	18. d	19. a	20. a
21. d	22. d	23. d	24. d	25. d	26. d	27. d	28. d	29. c	30. c
31. d	32. d	33. b	34. d	35. d	36. c	37. b	38. d	39. d	40. d
41. c	42. a	43. d	44. d	45. d	46. d	47. d	48. d	49. a	50. d
51. c	52. d	53. b	54. b						

Chapter 8

1. d	2. c	3. d	4. d	5. b	6. d	7. d	8. a	9. a	10. b
11. b	12. a	13. d	14. b	15. d	16. d	17. d	18. d	19. a	20. d
21. d	22. c	23. c	24. b	25. a	26. b	27. d	28. d	29. d	30. d
31. c	32. b	33. d	34. c						

Chapter 9

1. d	2. d	3. b	4. d	5. c	6. d	7. d	8. b	9. d	10. d
11. d	12. c	13. c	14. c	15. a	16. b	17. b	18. c	19. c	20. a
21. b	22. d	23. b	24. b	25. b	26. a	27. d	28. d	29. c	30. d
31. a	32. d	33. d	34. d	35. b	36. a	37. a	38. d	39. d	40. c
41. d	42. d	43. b							

Chapter 10

1. d	2. d	3. a	4. d	5. b	6. c	7. c	8. d	9. c	10. a
11. c	12. c	13. d	14. d	15. d	16. d	17. d	18. a	19. a	20. d
21. d	22. b	23. a	24. d	25. d	26. b	27. d	28. d	29. d	30. c
31. d	32. d	33. d	34. c	35. a	36. c	37. b	38. c	39. d	40. c
41. d	42. b	43. d							

Chapter 11

1. c	2. d	3. d	4. c	5. d	6. d	7. d	8. d	9. c	10. d
11. c	12. d	13. d	14. c	15. d	16. a	17. c	18. d	19. d	20. d
21. d	22. c	23. d	24. d	25. d	26. b	27. c	28. b	29. d	30. d
31. b	32. b	33. d	34. d	35. d	36. a	37. b	38. d	39. b	40. a
41. b									

Chapter 12

1. d	2. a	3. b	4. d	5. b	6. d	7. c	8. d	9. d	10. d
11. d	12. b	13. d	14. d	15. a	16. b	17. a	18. b	19. d	20. c
21. d	22. d	23. a	24. b	25. c	26. d	27. c	28. a	29. c	

ANSWER KEY

Chapter 13

1. b	2. b	3. b	4. d	5. a	6. d	7. d	8. d	9. a	10. c
11. d	12. d	13. d	14. d	15. c	16. d	17. b	18. c	19. d	20. c
21. d	22. d	23. d	24. a	25. d	26. d	27. d	28. d	29. d	30. d
31. a									

www.ingramcontent.com/pod-product-compliance
Lightning Source LLC
Chambersburg PA
CBHW082043230426
43670CB00016B/2755